Curtains

A Design Source Book

Curtains
A Design Source Book

Caroline Clifton-Mogg
photography by **James Merrell**

STEWART, TABORI & CHANG
NEW YORK

First published in 1997 by Ryland Peters & Small
Cavendish House, 51-55 Mortimer Street,
London W1N 7TD

Text copyright © 1997 by Caroline Clifton-Mogg
Design and illustration copyright © by 1997 Ryland Peters & Small

Published in 1997 and distributed by
Stewart, Tabori & Chang,
a division of U.S. Media Holdings, Inc.
115 West 18th Street, New York, New York 10011

Distributed in Canada by
General Publishing Company Ltd.
30 Lesmill Road
Don Mills, Ontario, M3B 2T6, Canada

Library of Congress Cataloging-in-Publication Data
Clifton-Mogg, Caroline.
    Curtains / by Caroline Clifton-Mogg ; photography by
James Merrell.
        p.   cm. – (A design source book)
    Includes index.
    ISBN 1-55670-603-0 (hardcover)
    1. Drapery-Handbooks, manuals, etc. I. Title. II.
Series.
NK3195.C62   1997
747'. 5–dc21   97-12775

Printed in Hong Kong
10 9 8 7 6 5 4 3 2 1

Designer   **Ingunn Cecilie Jensen**
Project Editor   **Caroline Davison**
Location Research   **Nadine Bazar**
Production   **Kate Mackillop**
DTP Manager   **Caroline Wollen**
Illustrators   **Jacqueline Pestell, Amanda Patton**
Art Director   **Jacqui Small**
Publishing Director   **Anne Ryland**

FRONT JACKET:
*James Merrell/Charles Chauliaguet and Françoise Dorget's apartment in Paris
by Caravane.*
BACK JACKET:
Above left: *James Merrell/design Françoise Gilles and Dominique
Lubar, IPL Interiors.*
Above right: *James Merrell/Mr. & Mrs. Patrick Frey.*
Below left: *Khai & Sue Kellet.*
Below right: *James Merrell/Mr. & Mrs. A'Court.*

Contents

FOREWORD

"Rich," "decorative," even "sumptuous": these are just some of the words used to describe the window treatments of the 1980s. Books of that decade reflected this mood and were crammed with photographs and illustrations of every type of drapery style and design. Today, there is a new attitude prevalent in interior design, a feeling that decoration can and should be much simpler, and that the excess that, to some extent, characterized the style of the last decade was just all too much. Perhaps this has something to do with the fact that over the last twenty years, and in particular over the last ten, there has been an increase in foreign travel, a pastime that has helped open our eyes to the ways in which others live and, more specifically, to how they use objects in their homes. Another relevant factor is that contemporary daily life has, for many people, become less settled and secure; there is now a feeling of movement and change. We move according to the location of our workplaces or in response to a change in our role in life. Therefore, it goes without saying that if you are going to move, your belongings, including any fabric furnishings, should be portable. Clearly, decorative simplicity is dictated by circumstance, and this is reflected in a more restrained mood in interior design.

So it is time for a new book on windows that once again answers questions on, and makes suggestions for, the simplest and most successful ways of dressing different windows, whatever their shape or size, and, in particular, focuses on treatments that reflect the spirit of the new, the fresh, and the simple.

Caroline Clifton-Mogg

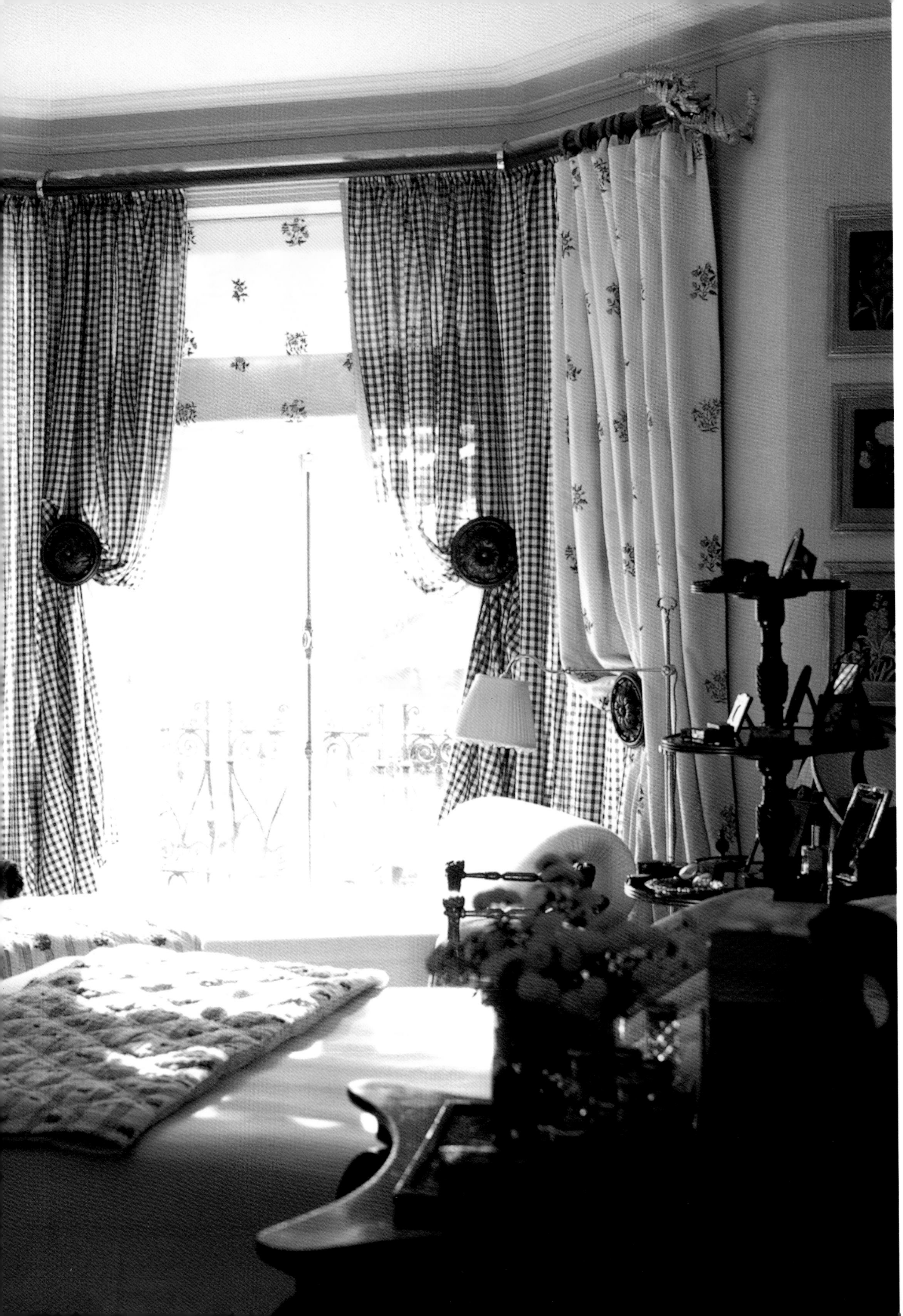

Influential Styles

BELOW, RIGHT, FAR RIGHT *Heavy, carved and gilded wooden cornices often surmounted equally heavy draperies. Here, in a Victorian house in London, a double-depth cornice is used with a traditional portière. Unusually, there are two draperies rather than one: the outer drapery is caught up with an ornamental rope while the lighter inner one is held back by a bracket hidden behind the outer draperies.*

Influential Styles

Taste, as commentators know to their cost, is almost impossible to define. In any group, taste is both personal and communal, formed not only by the influences on any one individual but also by the more general influences of society. In this time of instant communication, when we have immediate access to a wealth of inspirational sources, it is becoming increasingly difficult to define our personal tastes. This is why the styles of the past, particularly of draperies that reflect the interior decoration of a period so accurately, should be regarded as a well-stocked library of decorative treasures through which we can browse in search of inspiration. Indeed, the early 20th-century decorator John Fowler, who was renowned for his imaginative window treatments, gained much inspiration from 18th-century dress, and many were the draperies and swags to which he added a braided detail from an embroidered silk vest or a ruffle from a taffeta skirt. So let us document, briefly, the threads of fashion that, throughout the ages, have influenced, and can still lead to, new drapery styles.

As with every aspect of art, some periods have been more fruitful than others. Indeed, throughout the last few hundred years there has been imagination in drapery design from which we can draw inspiration as well as pleasure. Historically speaking, however, draperies have not always been perceived as a decorative element. In fact, it was not until humans had passed the stage of merely surviving that an appreciation of the beautiful in the natural world as well as in fine and decorative arts began to develop. Early householders had more pressing concerns, chief among them being how best to keep the cold and damp at bay. Textiles in the house were hung on the walls and around the bed rather than at the window—for practical rather than decorative reasons. But a love of decoration for its own sake is innate in humankind, and gradually even the early wall and bed hangings became richly ornate.

Draperies first came to notice as an essential element in interior decoration in 16th-century Europe. Inspiration came, as always at that time, from France and Italy, and the influence of these two bastions of fashion would be felt in England and the Low Countries some time later. The first draperies were single; pairs came later. The simplest consisted of strips of fabric, sometimes of basic weave and construction, somewhat like the natural curtain and drapery styles popular today. But other draperies were more flamboyant and made from velvets from Genoa or heavy brocades and silks from Venice.

By the 17th century, the technical problems in glazing windows had mainly been solved, and they gradually became larger. In England the draperies that hung at these vast windows were still rather basic, but elsewhere in Europe both window draperies and bed hangings became increasingly more elaborate. For example, the French designer Daniel Marot published ideas for extravagantly decorated beds which included huge drapes and swags, plumes and tassels, in an excess of richness. To a certain extent, the ideas of Marot and his contemporaries still influence decorative designs for headboards and canopies today, albeit in a simpler and, usually, more graceful form.

Beginning in 1700, a multiplicity of drapery styles began to appear, including the festoon curtain, which was the forerunner of our modern balloon or Austrian shade. When designed correctly and made in the right weight of material, these shades are a striking solution for a tall window. As with every other aspect of interior decoration and the decorative arts, the 18th century is, for many people, the period when drapery design reached its peak, never to be bettered in the future. Combining wit, imagination, and elegance, the draperies were relatively simple, straight, and made from beautiful materials. They hung from cornices and valances whose

ornamentation added to the whole effect and are still a yardstick by which to measure contemporary designs. Indeed, many of the styles and ideas proposed by architects and upholsterers of the time continue to influence modern draperies.

During the latter half of the 18th century and the early part of the 19th century, the neoclassical style became extremely popular. It remains so today in various forms. The first excavations of the lava-covered cities of Pompeii and Herculaneum in Italy also took place at this time. The paintings and mosaics on the walls and floors of the ancient houses in the ruins sparked off a long-lasting enthusiasm for classical architecture and decoration in Europe and America. From this period came drapery poles adorned with finials in the form of spears, laurel wreaths, and other militaristic or classical motifs which are popular today.

Indeed, the influence of the 18th-century Scottish designer Robert Adam, who was inspired by these classical designs and motifs,

is still great. He treated the draperies and the surrounding architrave, or window molding, particularly for the tall windows popular at the time, in a relatively simple manner with restrained swags and cascades or folded draw shades, which often fell from carved and gilded cornice boards made from wood or plaster. All these ideas and designs can be used in narrow-windowed rooms today.

By the end of the century, French-influenced draw draperies with a draped valance were also popular. They had a flowing line in which the material draped and billowed, offering opportunities for invention and inspiration. These draperies were made from lighter fabrics such as silks and cottons, taffetas and satins. No longer were draperies simply a means of controlling light: the dress curtain had arrived. Hung beneath valances in different designs, these draw draperies flowed from beneath a richly carved cornice board.

By the early 19th century the neoclassical look was refined once more. It became heavier, even ponderous, losing much of the lightness of touch used by Robert Adam. Great emphasis was placed on the decorative elements of design, in particular to the style of the valances, and swags and cascades. In fact, *passementerie*—all those lovely handmade fringes, tassels, braids, and rosettes—was as popular then as it is today.

FAR LEFT, ABOVE, LEFT *By the 19th century, a clearly definable, almost ponderous, quality had infiltrated the design and style of draperies. Very popular were deep valances that were set above draperies made from weighty materials. These draperies were usually braided, fringed, roped, and tasseled. In this Victorian house in London, a door drapery made from a richly colored fabric continues the feeling of rather heavy luxury. This is exemplified still further by the strength of the patterns on both the walls and the furniture.*

curtain or drapery at the window or several different sheers draped over a rod has a new relevance and can create very informal effects at windows.

However, by the 19th century the well-mannered simplicity of the past had gone. In both Europe and America the past was mined for inspiration, and earlier styles were revived with abandon—from the medieval to the Elizabethan, from Scottish Baronial to Louis X1V and Louis XV—and often used together. With this approach to style came a belief that a little more of everything was desirable. Drapery styles became rich in the extreme: so grand, so excessive, so much. New chemical dyes led to stronger, even harsher, colors, while window treatments consisting of heavy swags and cascades, outer draperies, inner draperies, sheer curtains, and often shades made from Holland linen were not unusual. No part of a room's architecture, including doorways, mantelpieces, and alcoves, remained free from drapery. If you wish to dress a window extravagantly, make sure that the finished design conveys a sense of vibrancy rather than of unbridled excess.

Toward the end of the 19th century, an inevitable reaction to the frills and fuss of High Victoriana took place, a development embodied by the Arts and Crafts movement. Designers and architects such as William

ABOVE, RIGHT In this modestly decorated room, the windows exhibit a simplified version of an often elaborate drapery style. Plain, relatively unadorned fabric is draped in an informal swag across a small window. Another piece of fabric is then arranged in a swag attached to the ceiling beams. Beneath this, an almost floor-length drapery is held back at sill height with a bracket.

FAR RIGHT This pair of unlined muslin curtains in Goethe's house in Weimar, through which the light gently shines, exemplifies the classic simplicity of the best of 18th-century design. The curtains are edged with passementerie *in the form of fringe and accompanied by a graceful swag.*

Drapery poles and finials often took center stage, seemingly artlessly draped with fabric in a number of imaginative ways. Two or more materials were often used at one window, combining not only different patterns but also varying textures and weights. Undercurtains of gauze or silk were also used; these either fell straight to the ground or were caught back, often in asymmetrical opposition to the accompanying draperies. Today, particularly with the wide selection of sheer fabrics now available, ranging from silk to synthetics, the idea of using more than one lightweight

Morris and Philip Webb advocated natural simplicity, whereby ornament became secondary to the object, not its *raison d'être*. They mocked the excesses of contemporary interior-decoration, and over the next few decades their ideas took hold, and rich, heavy furnishings became less common. Events far removed from design and decoration also influenced stylistic developments. During World War I, ornate draperies were regarded as impractical, and simpler designs, which were easier to keep clean and fresh, started to replace them. Following the war, such decorators as Nancy Lancaster, Sibyl Colefax, and John Fowler made a virtue of simplicity and began to decorate in what is now recognized as the style of the "English country house": comfortable, informal, and with relatively simpler, freer draperies.

Today, technical advances in fiber production and in printing have made the options almost infinite. So, whether you prefer restrained 18th-century-inspired narrow draperies, full-blown draperies and swags, unlined muslin and silk suspended from a wooden pole, or even electronically controlled Venetian blinds, all is possible, all is attainable.

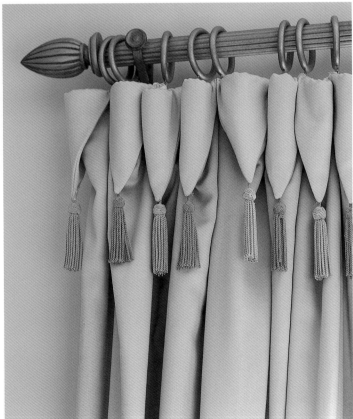

LEFT, ABOVE *These relatively simple draperies are a contemporary version of a popular Regency design. The ornamental reeded brass pole is typical of many early 19th-century designs, while the shape of the finials can be seen in many neoclassic illustrations. A drapery heading of elongated handkerchief points, edged with tassels in two colors, emphasizes the curves of the finials.*

19

Window Style

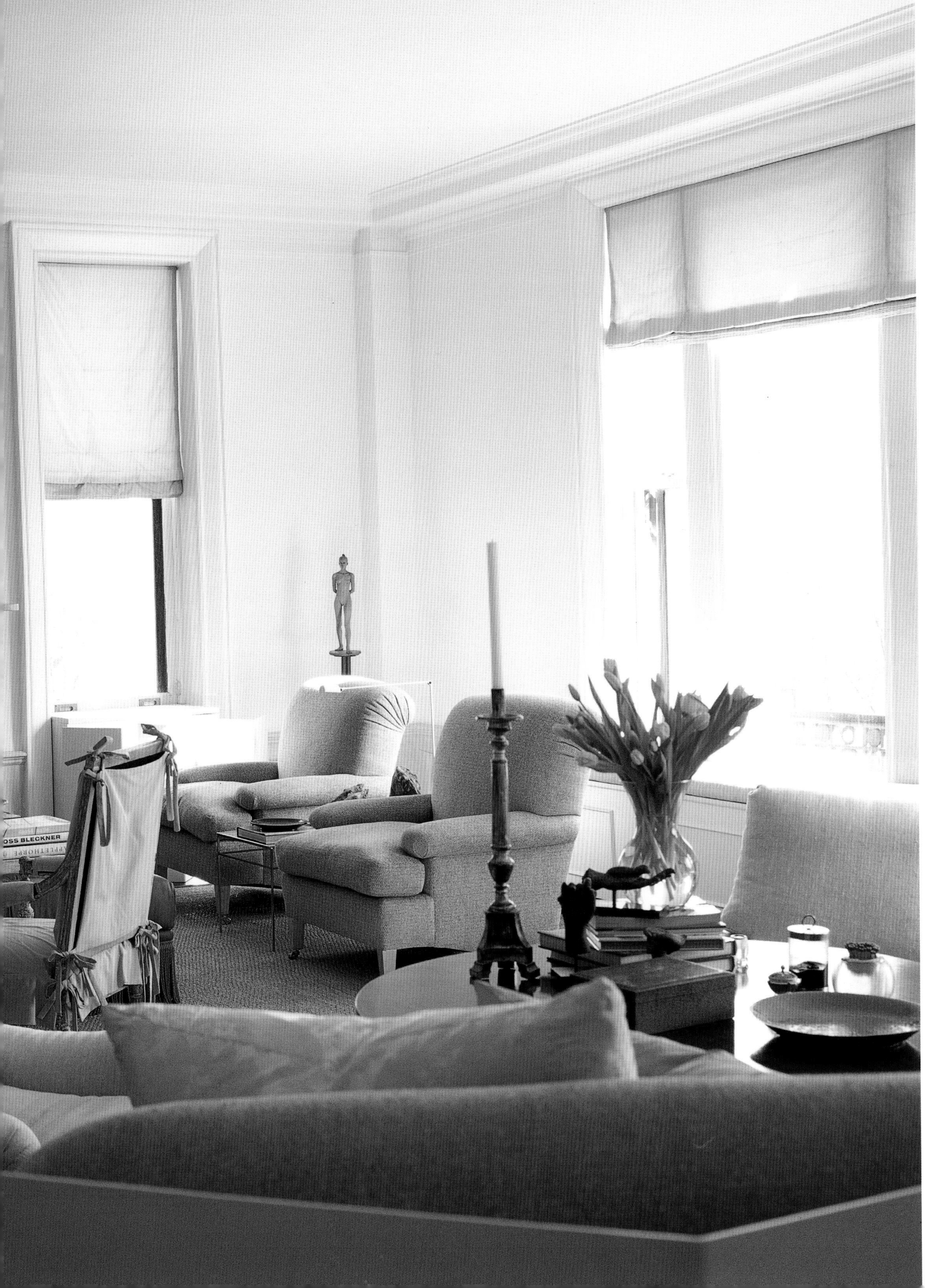

WINDOW STYLE

Whether conventionally beautiful or simply practical, every window has a unique character that is integral to the architectural style and interior design of the house. People need light and air, and when they enter a room for the first time, their eyes are usually drawn to the window, whether it is dressed with traditional draperies; shades made from fabric, wood, metal, plastic, or paper; fretwork, paper, or trellis screens; painted stencils; or even climbing plants. But it is only by standing back and looking at your uncovered windows that you will be able to study their shape and assess their individual merits and needs. Whatever the size of the window, it should be dressed to look as appealing as possible and never hidden beneath a torrent of fabric. Instead, the window should remind you of a beautiful woman at a party whose understated gown ensures everyone finds her as enchanting as her dress.

ABOVE *These windows are dressed as one, in such a way that they dominate the room. The sheer draperies are caught back in a deep loop at the same point as the heavier outer draperies. The effect would not be so successful were it not for the obelisk which draws the windows together.*

RIGHT *As this drapery, which is mainly plain except for the plaid heading, shows, a drapery can also be used to good effect on a wall.*

RIGHT *An awkwardly placed window such as this, which reaches into the corner of the room, leaves little space for draperies on either side or even above. However, the draperies, which are slotted over a shiny metal pole through oversized metal eyelets, are particularly arresting. The area is made more interesting by the mirrored wall, which emphasizes the window treatment by doubling its size. The elegant chair in front of the window blends in color with the draperies.*

Tall Windows

A tall window, especially one of fine proportions, is an object of style. Particularly associated with the Georgian architecture and style of the 18th century—a period commonly acknowledged to have epitomized all that is elegant in decoration—such windows are a perfection of design. If any of your rooms has classic proportions and is blessed with tall windows, you are lucky indeed, and a variety of styles can be yours.

In British Georgian houses the tallest windows are usually found on the second floor. Traditionally known as the *piano nobile*, this is where the formal reception rooms were situated. Today, such rooms and windows offer bounteous opportunities for both traditional, formal treatments and simpler designs. Treatments for tall windows should concentrate on maximizing the available light. This is perhaps obvious, but in an enthusiasm for complicated designs it is sometimes ignored. So, even if yours is a very tall window in a classically proportioned room, show some restraint in your choice of drapery style, and avoid draperies, valances, swags and cascades, or cornice boards that are too heavy or ornate.

Although a tight, restrained look is chic, narrow draperies must be made with enough

ABOVE, ABOVE LEFT *The whole of this tall, narrow window is dressed with a single drapery panel, caught back with a rope that is attached to the window frame. The shape of this window offers an ideal opportunity to use a piece of old textile, in this case an antique paisley shawl, and provides a perfect frame for the deep border and traditional motifs.*

FAR LEFT, TOP CENTER *This tall window butts up to a wood-clad ceiling, and so the drapery heading is necessarily a simple one. A wrought-iron pole is fixed directly to the bare wood, and the draperies are hung from rings that are attached to the deceptively simple fold-over heading. The blue ribbons, which pick out the color of the draperies, are tied into bows in front of each ring.*

fabric to make their fullness look intentionally restricted rather than the result of parsimony. If you have a period house, consider when it was built and how the original owners would have treated the windows. What could be more appropriate than a pair of classic draperies headed with a simple swag and cascades or a single panel draped diagonally across the window frame and caught high up with a tieback or a metal bracket? This last treatment is also a smart way to dress a window with interior shutters.

If you would prefer not to have a valance or swags and cascades at a tall window, then the type and depth of the drapery heading you choose is of the utmost importance. You can opt for basic pinch pleats, formed with special pleat tape and hooks, or drawstrings, or you can indulge your taste for elegance with a hand-sewn heading in one of a variety of styles, from the simple to the elaborate. Unless you are confident of your measuring and sewing skills, however, a complex design should be entrusted to a professional. Fortunately, many of the most fashionable headings are simple, with the fabric softly pleated or even left flat, and well within the capabilities of an amateur.

BELOW LEFT *Here, where there is no wall space between the windows and the ceiling molding and where the windows also extend to the very corners of the room, only the simplest treatment is possible, with the draperies suspended by rings from an unadorned iron pole.*

BOTTOM LEFT *This room has a "dead" space above the window, although the draperies hanging below the pole give an illusion of space.*

BELOW *Here, there is little space between the fairly thick architrave and ceiling. To minimize bulk, the draperies are flat panels, hung by brass grommets from a specially designed, gently undulating pole. The effect is soft yet striking.*

The section of the window from which you hang draperies or curtains always requires some thought, particularly with a tall window, because a rod hung in the wrong position can alter its proportions, sometimes for the worse. The usual choice is on the architrave or just above, but if the rod is hung above the window, you should make sure that no molding or cornice is obscured. Ideally, as in most old houses, there is often a section of wall between the top of the window frame and the cornice, known in Britain as the deadlight. However, in badly converted or modern

ABOVE *This badly proportioned window with no space above it has been salvaged by hanging the draperies from a metal pole and attaching a wide swath of fabric which is deliberately allowed to sag in the center. This creates an attractive, draped effect that draws the eye away from the area above the window.*

FAR RIGHT *A tall, narrow window in a paneled room is hung with a single, striped drapery from a classical pole. The unusual textile with a thick black border, which flows over much of the drapery, not only breaks up its height but is also an original decorative device.*

versions of classic rooms, there is often no such space. In this case, the proportions of both window and drapery should be righted optically if not physically after the rod has been attached. This can sometimes be done with a valance or cornice that, rather than cutting horizontally across the window, follows the window down on either side, thus bringing the eye downward too. A plain, full-height, translucent shade that hangs from beneath the draperies will also anchor the window and prevent it appearing to float in the wall space.

One way to allow as much light as possible through a tall window, while still showing off its fine lines, is to use a draw-up blind. These were originally popular in the 17th and 18th centuries, when windows began to sport festoon curtains, made in translucent materials such as muslin or silk or in damask or figured silk. Such shades were hung either beneath formal stationary panels or from a cornice board made from carved and gilded wood or plaster. These elegant panels were also eminently practical because they could be drawn up underneath the cornice in order to allow in the maximum amount of light.

The modern balloon shades are far less dignified, however. In Britain they are often referred to derogatorily as "knicker [panty] blinds," because of the preponderance of overly large frills. Balloon shades today are all too often seen hanging against unsuitably shaped windows, which are either too wide, too small, or too tall, and are often made from inappropriate fabrics and in unsuitable designs. It is a shame that this style is so badly handled when it still has a perfectly useful role to play under the right circumstances, namely at a tall window where space is limited. In short, if you employ a treatment that is in itself elaborate, no embellishment to the basic shape is really necessary. The basic shape of the shade itself should be simple, with the trimmings kept to a minimum. When you pull

ABOVE *The proportions of a window that is not full height can be improved by designing a special window treatment. Here, narrow draperies are tied back at sill height, which carries the eye downward, as does the gently curved valance. This gives the draperies more impact than the window.*

BELOW *A badly proportioned window is corrected with a witty treatment in which the draperies fold over a loose rope secured by brackets. This draws the attention away from the window, while the way in which the draperies flow over the floor balances the weight at ceiling level.*

All this advice holds true for perfectly proportioned windows, but sadly, in an often less than ideal decorative world, even such seemingly simple features as a window of perfect proportions are hard to find. Windows are often too narrow, too wide, or simply too tall for the height of the room. In such cases, care must be taken to balance any proportional problems in order to achieve the best effects. If the window is too narrow, the simplest solution is to extend the rod beyond the window frame so that the draperies hang against the wall rather than the architrave. Tall, narrow windows can be made to look wider with the addition of louvered or paneled shutters which, when not in use, hinge backward so that they rest flat against the walls on each side of the window rather than folding back into the recess.

A tall, narrow window does not, of course, always extend to floor level. If this is your situation make sure that you use the draperies to correct this by taking the draperies to floor level and maybe using a contrasting band of fabric at the bottom of each panel. You could also paint a panel on the dead area of wall above the floor. Both these treatments have the effect of anchoring and extending the window.

Narrow windows on the same wall can be dressed to look wider, while still admitting the maximum amount of light, by adding a false valance. This is achieved by attaching a valance or an arrangement of swags to the draperies themselves rather than to the window frame. When the draperies are opened, the valances draw back with them; when closed, they look like richly dressed hangings.

However, not every pair of draperies at a tall window needs to open. Indeed, if you have a tall window on a landing or at a turn in the stairs, carefully draped stationary panels left permanently in their show position will look much better than draperies that are constantly being adjusted.

ABOVE *These windows are awkwardly sited, with one in a corner of the room and the other very nearby. But a virtue is made of this proximity by hanging both windows with the same vibrantly colored draperies. Large squares of bright color are sewn together in order to create an eye-catching, sheer patchwork effect. The fabric blocks that make up the draperies also echo the other rectangular shapes in the room.*

down the shade on a tall window, make sure that the area on display is in proportion to that of the window below. Another option for such a well-proportioned window is a flat-pleated Roman shade which is usually hung within the window frame, its horizontal fold lines displaying the architecture of the window.

BELOW, RIGHT, FAR RIGHT *A simple, intrinsically uninteresting window is made to look both wider and more important by a dramatic window treatment which also allows maximum light to enter the room. Behind the pole, a curtain made from a sheer yellow fabric is slipped over a curtain rod and then caught back by a hidden tieback. The heavier drapery, which is suspended from the pole, is arranged to produce a narrow, more formal drape.*

FAR LEFT, LEFT, ABOVE *This is a contemporary version of a classic window treatment in which a modern fabric design with wide, strongly colored stripes hangs from beneath an ornate, gilded cornice. This gives the drapery as much weight as the cornice. These are particularly well-chosen draperies for landings because they add much to the lines of the staircase as well as promote a feeling of security and comfort.*

Wide Windows

Improvements in glass-making technology over the past few centuries have made possible a huge variety of window styles. In the 17th and 18th centuries, windows were composed of many small panes, and it was not until the introduction of plate glass in the 19th century that window sashes made of a single large pane could be manufactured. As glazing costs fell, windows grew wider as well as taller.

Wide or large windows made from several panes of glass can be treated in a different manner from those used for single-paned windows. For example, multipaned windows can be effectively dressed with blinds or shades or hung with floor-length draperies. You can also introduce some contrast within the glazing by using opaque glass for some of the panes in order to produce an abstract design.

The treatment of large picture windows can be problematic. If the house is secluded, it may be possible to leave such a window uncovered, so as to bring the view into the room. But if your neighbors have a view of you, some form of curtaining is vital. This also helps to conserve heat and reduce fading of carpets and furniture. The trick is to achieve this without suggesting that the "big show" is about to begin.

One of the first considerations is whether you want the draperies to be full length or sill length. Once again, it is a question of proportion: width must always be balanced by height, and if the window is wider than it is high, the width should be balanced with sufficient fabric length below the window—or even with fabric extended above the window. If you need to break up the glazed area visually, two or three flat, pleated Roman shades or an equal number of roller shades that are set at different heights along the window should have the desired effect.

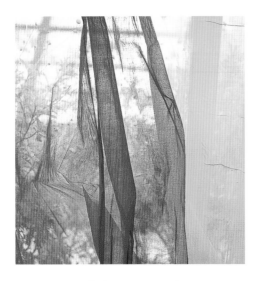

FAR LEFT, BOTTOM CENTER *Wide windows almost always present problems of proportion, especially if they do not extend from the ceiling to the floor. Here, a shallow, wide window is cleverly dressed with two Roman shades. These are set at different heights for added variety and interest, as is shown in the smaller detail. Made of sheer fabric, the Roman shades can be kept partially raised at any level across the width of the window. This treatment is successful because it breaks up what would otherwise be a rather unattractive expanse of glass. The border that has been stitched down the sides and along the bottom of each shade is almost the same width as the dark window frames. This creates a highly harmonious effect.*

BELOW, LEFT, TOP CENTER *Typical picture windows can be rather overwhelming by virtue of their sheer size, seeming to dominate the room in which they are situated. This is particularly obvious when the windows occupy two walls. The clever solution devised here turns a series of windows into an ethereal fantasy with sheer gauzelike draperies in wide rainbow-colored stripes. These draperies fall in a relaxed, unstructured fashion, and billow in the breeze. The informality of the treatment is emphasized further by the almost casual heading style of the curtains. This consists of pieces of string tied into loose decorative bows. The effect is one of impermanence that suits the relaxed atmosphere of the room.*

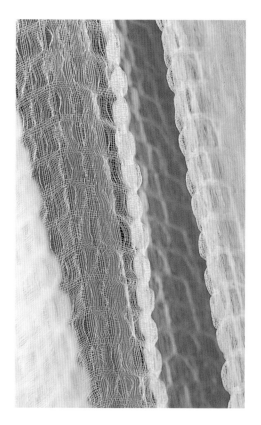

Similarly, if you would like to diminish the area of a window, you could use a lambrequin, which, somewhat like an extended valance, runs down either side of the window as well as across the top. By positioning the lambrequin over a section of the window, you can lessen the area of glass visible from inside the room.

If you have a wide window, it is tempting to hang an elaborate confection of swags and cascades across the top. Try not to succumb to this temptation. First, it is difficult to successfully design an arrangement of swags across such a wide area, and second, you should really try to focus attention on the view offered by such an expanse of glass rather than on the draperies around the view. Simplicity in this case is definitely the best approach. If the view is beautiful, consider having the curtains blend with the color of the walls, so that the landscape, not the interior decoration, becomes predominant.

Whatever your view, however, the design of fabric for any large expanse of glass, whether it is composed of a single window or the entire width so that a diffusion of, or even a mere suggestion of, the world outside is all that permeates. For example, muslin or a fine voile looks good, particularly if it has a woven rather than printed design. Decorative lace, with its delicacy and intricate detail, would be less successful over a large window area—a little of such a fabric goes a long way. A more flexible alternative would be to fix a sequence of paper screens across the window. These would not only diffuse the light but also break up the space occupied by the glass.

OPPOSITE (bottom, top left, top center) *The drapery fabric at these wide windows has a strong surface interest. The heavy, rippled fabric is used in profusion to create sculptural folds. The severity of the treatment is softened by the gentle puddling of the draperies on the floor.*

BELOW, LEFT, OPPOSITE (top right) *These wide windows are hung with draperies made from a dimpled, plastic fabric. The draperies are headed with pleats that are seemingly held together with ties and run on a barely visible rod.*

a group of windows, should be chosen with care. It should be neither too subdued nor too elaborate, because a design that is charming over an average-sized space can be a disaster when repeated ad infinitum. Small, indeterminate prints, stripes, or plaids simply will not work. Large windows call for equally large and flamboyant designs, whether they be naturalistic, abstract, geometric, or striped.

Solid-colored fabrics work well, but if the expanse to be covered is exceptionally large, a drapery would probably look better if it is defined by wide, contrasting borders that run down the edges or across the lower edge. A valance or cornice will also add definition to draperies made from solid-colored fabric. Of course, if the view from your window is not appealing, you can use a sheer material across

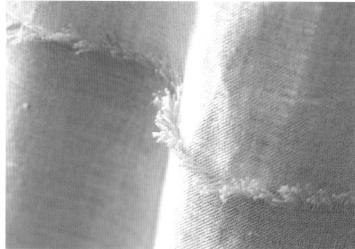

LEFT, ABOVE, RIGHT *Tall, wide windows often need an optical illusion to bring them into scale. Here, the inner draperies start some way down from the top of the window, suspended by strings fixed above the window. Righting the balance, but extending the illusion, another drapery is hung from the ceiling and reaches farther into the room. The draperies are made from wide bands of coarse material sewn together in an informal way.*

BELOW *A traditional treatment for a picture window that does not cover the length of the room is simply to extend the draperies beyond the window onto the wall itself. This simple procedure cohesively unites wall, window, and room.*

When choosing a fabric for wide windows, you should also consider how the amount of light that filters through the material will influence the whole effect. For example, a thick lining material, which admits very little light, would draw attention to the design of a drapery fabric. By contrast, unlined draperies have a slightly translucent look which can be particularly pretty when the draperies are made of such material as silk or light cotton.

Some picture windows, especially those that are situated at first floor level, are part fixed glass and part sliding door. When deciding on the type of curtains or draperies for this arrangement, you should make sure that they can be pulled back beyond the sliding mechanism of the door so that the folds of material do not get caught when you open or shut the door.

Many of the suggestions made so far apply to windows that are reasonably well proportioned. Unfortunately, there are many wide windows that have been less skillfully designed. Indeed, they seem to lack any sense of composition or proportion, simply resembling faceless expanses of glass. In addition, ill-designed wide windows are often not helped by ugly frames, usually made from metal, which are meagerly proportioned. However, badly proportioned wide windows can be corrected to some extent by the judicious use of window treatments.

FAR LEFT, LEFT, BELOW *In a bedroom, care must be taken not to overwhelm the room with the window treatment. Here, a window is visually enlarged by extending the pole and draperies beyond the sides of the window. The finished effect is not heavy, however, due to the simple design of the material and the traditional, almost anonymous, style of the drapery pole.*

OPPOSITE *Wide, shallow windows can be effectively treated with shades, particularly if they look unusual. Here, a single piece of cocoa-colored fabric, which is less formal than a traditional Roman shade, is supported by strips of ribbon tied into bows along the bottom. Decorative metal hooks provide an unusual finishing touch.*

For example, the apparent size of the window can, if necessary, be extended with headings or poles that run beyond the windows themselves so that the draperies hang down the wall on either side of the window rather than cutting into the window.

If the window is disproportionately tall, a fixed cornice board of a suitable depth would correct the height. More than two curtains could be hung from behind the board at various points to give the impression, when opened, of separate windows.

As is the case for wide windows that have perfect proportions, three or four flat, pleated shades can be used successfully to break up the area of glass, reduce the levels of light, and provide an element of privacy. Indeed, the many shade systems now available are the ideal solution for wide windows. Shades have the added advantage of being highly flexible treatments. They also vary considerably in style and price, from the relatively cheap to the extremely expensive. A low-looped, sheer Austrian shade, for example, could be pulled down permanently over part of the window, perhaps beneath a pair of draperies. This would diffuse the light and also alter the proportions of the window.

Small Windows

Many houses and apartments have small windows and, as with other windows with a distinctive shape, the first question to be asked is whether they should be covered at all. This is probably not advisable if the window is set high in the wall. Indeed, a small, uncovered window can be a decorative feature in itself, especially if the wooden frame is painted in an eyecatching, and perhaps contrasting, color. If there is a deep sill, this could also be painted to emphasize the shape of the window further.

A sense of scale is very important when dealing with small windows, and decorative ideas must be in proportion to the size of the window. You should avoid, for example, such embellishments as drooping swags and cascades or any of the other more exaggerated headings that work so well on larger windows. Headings should not be too deep, and if you are using a decorative rod, make sure that it is thin enough to match the weight and depth of the curtain or drapery. Small windows do not even need two panels. A single panel caught back to form a loop on one side of the

ABOVE *A tiny window is given a new importance with a clever treatment. A piece of material is draped from an iron pole, suspended above the window, to from a heavy swag which, although imposing, allows in the maximum amount of light.*

TOP, ABOVE LEFT *Just because a window is small does not mean it has to be dull. Here, in a charming variation of an asymmetrical Georgian swag, a floor-length, white drapery is caught back beneath the sill, which has the effect of elongating the window. The drapery is crowned with a heavy, striped material which, with its rough, scalloped edge, suggests both a valance and a classic swag and cascades.*

window is a pretty and practical idea. The drapery can be released at night or kept in place, with a plain shade to keep out the light.

Often out of proportion to the wall or room, small windows require a dextrous treatment to counteract any design fault. If, for example, the window is narrow as well as short, the drapery rod should be extended so that the draperies hang on either side of the frame. However, make sure that the rod extends only a little way on each side so that there is no wall space visible between the draperies and the window frame.

Small windows are often hung with sill-length draperies or curtains because floor-length panels usually look out of proportion. But if you are trying to correct uneven proportions, the length could be extended an inch or two below the sill; alternatively, the rod might be set slightly higher, usually without losing the sense of scale. If you do want to hang floor-length draperies over a small window, perhaps to correct the proportions of

LEFT, BELOW *Unlined draperies are ideal for small windows, particularly if there are also shutters. This pretty fabric, embroidered with a trail of flowers along the top, is tied back and draped beyond the window frame in order to maximize the amount of light in the room.*

the rest of the room, you should consider positioning both the draperies and a roller shade well above the window. The roller shade can then be pulled down to cover the exposed wall and part of the window to give the appearance of a much larger window.

If the small window is set into a recess, the window could be hung with a roller shade and the wall that opens to the recess itself might be hung with a pair of floor-length draperies. These could perhaps be made in a material that complements the blind. This gives not only the window but also the whole area a new importance. Another solution, if you have a small window set into a deep recess, is to repeat the design of the window frame

around the outer edge of the window in order to create the illusion of a much larger window. You could emphasize the effect still further by painting both the frame and the outer frame in a contrasting color.

If the small window is also rather ugly—and this applies equally to unattractive large or narrow windows—then one solution is to dress them as insignificantly as possible and to harmonize the color of the curtains or draperies with the color of the walls. Try using fabric one tone paler or darker than the color of the walls to create a harmonious look without drawing too much unwanted attention to the window. It goes without saying that the window treatment in such a case should not

BELOW LEFT *These bedroom windows combine several problems: one of the windows is small and also curved at the top, while the other is set into a sloping wall. The first window is flanked by sheer curtains that extend well beyond the window and covered with a roller shade set above the curve. The light through the other window is diffused by a sheer curtain hung from a narrow rod.*

BELOW *This tiny, oval window is imaginatively treated with a curtain pierced with grommets hung from a narrow rod; ornamental metal hooks are set along the top of the window frame. The finished result is utterly charming.*

BOTTOM *Multicolored ribbons are attached to a fixed, narrow rod set against the window itself. The architrave frames the composition.*

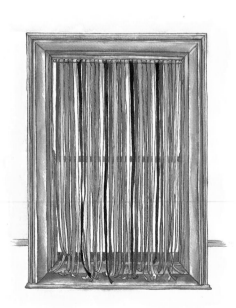

be overly elaborate. If the treatment is simple and straightforward, the curtains or draperies—and the windows themselves—will make their presence felt in only the most well-mannered of ways.

Your choice of fabric is also very important. As a rule, you should avoid heavy velvets, brocades, wools, and heavily embossed cottons. Small windows require light, airy materials which both reflect and balance their diminutive size. The same rule applies to patterned fabrics, which should be simpler in design and scale than those used at larger windows. When seen in a pattern book or in a shop, the design of a fabric, particularly if it

has a petite repeating pattern, will look much smaller than the finished curtain, drapery, or shade fitted at the window.

This is an appropriate moment to explore the advantages of using colored linings at undersized windows. Indeed, a small window curtained in fabric that has a simple, little design and a lining in one of the colors in the design, or in a soft, welcoming color such as deep pink or warm yellow, brings a feeling of comfort and coziness to the bleakest of days, seeming to change the color of the light inside the room. Such a treatment also gives the window a cheerful appearance from outside the house.

ABOVE, ABOVE LEFT *A Roman shade is one of the cleanest and neatest ways of treating a small window. Here, the shade is set within the architrave, and the edges are trimmed with fabric in a contrasting stripe.*

TOP CENTER *This small window, beneath which there is some rather attractive paneling, is an ideal candidate for an original piece of material. Suspended by rings from an iron pole set above the window, the fabric is caught back high enough so as not to detract from the overall shape.*

FAR LEFT (top, bottom) *This stagecoach shade is unlined but bordered with a contrasting fabric. The wide strips that support the shade break up the window and culminate in two large bows.*

Shades also work very well at small windows. They can be raised easily, which means that they do not obscure the available light. Roller shades, by virtue of their simple lines, are probably the best choice for small windows. A correctly proportioned Roman shade is also suitable, but the full sweep of an Austrian or balloon shade is usually overwhelming for a small window. Shades also provide an ideal opportunity for using a contrasting binding or border around the edge. Not only does this look dramatic, but it also defines the window and prevents it from seeming to float in the surrounding wall space. If you wish to maximize the window area, remember that shades can be hung outside as well as inside the window frame.

ABOVE, LEFT *Heavily textured Roman shades give a clean look to a boldly decorated room. The frame is painted white to contrast with the striped panels on the walls.*

CENTER *Traditional café curtains set halfway down these casement windows allow a modicum of privacy. Slipped over a narrow rod, they bring a countrylike atmosphere to the room.*

FAR LEFT (top) *Small windows in rooms with low ceilings require simple treatments, particularly when there are also heavy beams. Here, narrow draperies are tied to a metal pole.*

FAR LEFT (bottom) *These curtains are slipped over rods that are attached to the tops of the windows. The delicate braid that edges the curtains enhances the rural charm of the whole picture.*

Today, French windows and doors that open directly onto a balcony or into a garden are a delightful asset to a house or an apartment, bringing the outdoors inside in a charming and unique way. Depending on where in a room they are situated, they do not always need curtaining. Also, if the design is pleasing in itself, curtains of any type would be excessive. In this case, you could either leave them completely plain or hang an informal swag of sheer material or an antique textile over a pole that stretches across the top of the window.

If a French window does not stand alone but is, as so often happens, in the center of a pair of fixed windows, or if it matches other windows on another wall in the room, all the windows should be treated in the same fashion. They should be dressed with full-length draperies that are simple in concept and design. In addition, a single drapery is really preferable for a French window for practical reasons, and you should then try to tie in the design with the other more conventional windows

LEFT, BELOW, RIGHT *This classically perfect set of French windows demands a classically perfect window treatment. Balloon shades were, in fact, originally designed for tall windows such as these. Here, they hang in perfect proportion to the rest of the room. The informally gathered shade above the French windows is set high enough so as not to impede the movement of the doors, while the two smaller windows on either side are dressed with smaller gathered shades. Both these smaller shades are balanced by an inner shade that is beautifully edged with an ebullient fringe.*

French Windows and Doors

French doors are so called, not surprisingly, because of their extensive use in French houses, particularly in first-floor rooms and important second-floor rooms where full-height glazed doors were an essential part of the architectural plan. They grew in popularity across Europe during the late 18th and early 19th centuries, reflecting the leisured, pleasurable way of life pursued by many at that time and exemplifying the development of windows over the centuries as objects of beauty in their own right.

In the past, and particularly on the Continent, French windows, or doors, were often emphasized with a stiffened lambrequin or woven portière, which followed the lines of the window down the frame and often reached all the way to the floor. If your French windows stand alone, unencumbered by other windows, a contemporary version of one of these styles would be very striking. It might take the form of a shaped plywood frame that is painted, stenciled, or covered with fabric. Alternatively, a conventional stiffened valance could be made to extend farther down the sides of the window. Needless to say, any draperies hung beneath such dramatic frames should be simple in style and made in a relatively plain fabric.

in the room. Somewhat like a bay window, the French windows and the side windows can be unified by whatever you hang over the top. Indeed, if the frame around the door is a beautiful feature in itself, just drape a piece of eye-catching textile across a pole, either symmetrically or, even better, asymmetrically.

French windows may open outward or inward. If they open inward, the rod or pole must extend far enough beyond the edges of the window to allow the doors to open without obstruction. Should you need more privacy, sheers can be used within the door frames or hung from the top of the frame. They can also be attached at both the top and bottom of the frame with a cased heading on adjustable narrow metal curtain rods. Loosely woven sheer fabrics such as muslin look better folded into loose pleats, or gathered slightly, than stretched taut across the frame.

Shades also work particularly well at French windows—with the possible exception of Austrian or balloon shades, whose fullness and slightly exaggerated style make them

BELOW LEFT *A simple solution for French windows in an informal room is to hang the curtains or draperies at a distance from the opening. Here, extended brackets support a rod onto which a pair of unlined curtains is slipped.*

BELOW, BOTTOM *A multidimensional approach for French windows or glazed doors is to treat each window separately with narrow roller or Roman shades and to unite the two with a set of draperies on a pole. Here, the shades are in crewel-work, which is an unusual choice, and the outer draperies are sheer, partly to reveal the shades.*

ABOVE, RIGHT *Glazed doors are not always set flush with the wall, and those with a deep recess need a treatment that will encompass the return. Here, a curved rail allows the draperies, with their neat pinch pleats, to completely obscure the architrave.*

LEFT *A pair of glazed doors is treated with full-length draperies made with grommets, which are slotted over a pole and tied back halfway down the door. Because the window is in a corner, a separate drapery serves the same function as a stationary panel, adding further importance to the whole scheme.*

largely unsuitable because they interfere with the mechanism of opening and shutting. They will also distract from the vertical lines of the window. Roman and roller shades are a much better proposition, particularly if they are used at French windows that are set within a large bank of other windows because the shades can be set at different heights in order to add variety and interest to the window shapes. The shades could be made from a solid-colored fabric and perhaps edged with a border to define them within the window space; if you prefer a patterned material, you will find that stripes or plaids are much more effective than allover or floral designs.

Often a French window is less a window and more a glazed door leading onto a balcony or terrace. If it stands alone, it can be dressed like a conventional French window, but if it is flanked by a pair of smaller windows, which do not extend to floor level, simply structured Venetian blinds may be the answer, with long blinds used for the door, short ones for the windows. When lowered, they will unify the windows in a manner that is not possible with curtains or draperies.

ABOVE, RIGHT *When the French windows are particularly large, avoid large expanses of the same fabric. These full-size French windows are hung with alternate lengths of contrasting material. With so much interest in the fabric itself, there is no need for an elaborate heading.*

LEFT, TOP *At a pair of French windows that is not opened very often an alternative idea is simply to attach two lengths of fabric to the window frame using hooks, rings, and nails instead of brackets. One of the panels may then be tied back in order to let in air and light.*

Bay and Bow Windows

Some people feel that a bay window is difficult to treat, but in fact, as long as each window within the bay is treated in a similar fashion, all is simplicity itself. This applies even if there is a relatively large area of wall between each window. The number of windows in a bay ranges from three to six or seven, and the curtains or draperies can either follow the angled shape or run across the bay to create a flat projection; this is often done in a modern-style house. A bay window also increases the levels of light and the sense of space in a room, so if you are lucky enough to have one, regard it as a bonus rather than an irritant.

If your bay window is fairly flat and there is room within the recess, a single drapery panel on either side of the area should suffice. Bay windows also often have an expanse of wall within the bay, in which case you should place two narrow panel draperies on either side to cover the wall along with a pair of functional draw draperies across the window itself. With a large surface area of glass, a single pair of draperies is too bulky and heavy for the window, as well as difficult to close. In this case, it would be much better to hang at least two panels between the separate windows and place the rods over the architraves.

You can unite the different windows within a bay by hanging sheer draperies over the whole window area, or alternatively by putting shades over each window and uniting them with a set of panel draperies at strategic points. For angled bays, which probably make up the majority

of bay windows, you will need a cut-to-measure rod, which is widely
available. You can either use angled rods, which follow the contours of
the window, or, alternatively, continuous, curved rods attached to either
the wall or the ceiling.

During the 18th and 19th centuries, bay windows were often
headed with a heavy valance with draw draperies hanging below.
Indeed, a bay is the one window on which some kind of continuous
heading is almost essential, uniting the individual windows and the
draperies. It should not be overly elaborate or concealed beneath an
excess of frippery. The heading needs to be specially designed and
possibly geometrically angled. A particularly dramatic effect can be
achieved by fixing a wooden cornice board that has been cut in a
continuous curve to follow the bay around. This would transform the
window from an area of squared angles to one of flowing curves.

Rooms with bay windows are not always well proportioned, which
means that the bay appears at odds with the rest of the room, further
affecting its overall shape. If this is the case, you could design the
draperies as if they were part of a theatrical stage, cutting straight across

LEFT *The treatment of this shallow bay window, which is dressed with
smart blue-and-white striped draperies, is held together by a boldly shaped
valance as well as by full-length draperies on the left and right. These are
made in the same striped material as the window draperies and used to cover
the contents of two shelving units.*

ABOVE, LEFT, RIGHT *These draperies on a bay window in a period house are headed with deep smocking. Set beneath a continuous cornice, the carving of which resembles the smocked heading, the central draperies are caught together, while the outer draperies are held back with decorative pegs. The material of which the draperies are made is beautifully edged with tiny, subtly colored tassels.*

OPPOSITE *Resembling an oversized party dress, these draperies, with an elegant heading are ideal for a shallow bay window. The dramatic treatment is continued with the tiebacks, which are nearly at floor level and encourage the bottom of the draperies to sink gracefully to the floor.*

the opening so that the bay window is hidden when the draperies are closed. The area within the bay window could be separated still further from the rest of the room by furnishing it with comfortable chairs and a small table, which would give it a different function, perhaps as a writing alcove or a reading room.

Sometimes a bay is not the only window along the wall of a room. The bay window is often at the front of the house with another

smaller window nearby. However, both windows can be united with draperies that have the same heading or even a cornice or valance that runs across them both, including the alcove of the bay. This arrangement requires only the lightest of touches as far as the valance or cornice is concerned. In such a case, and for a single bay window where the

bay is particularly deep, you might like to consider installing a window seat. This would not only anchor the bay window in a confident manner but also suggest a feeling of leisure, especially if the seat were fitted with soft cushions made either in the same fabric as the draperies or at least in a material that complements them. You could pile some large

ABOVE, TOP RIGHT *This bay window is unified by using the black border material to make a separate knotted tassel to hang from the center of each window. There is further decorative interest in the fact that whereas the draperies themselves are longer than usual, the knotted tassels extend down to sill level.*

RIGHT *As a way of breaking up the impact of a bay window, these draperies are designed with a very deep, contrasting band of fabric that makes the windows, and the draperies themselves, look shorter than they actually are.*

pillows on top of the seat to make the area in front of the bay window even more inviting.

Bow windows have always been admired and treated with much care, their pretty shape being a delightful sight from both inside and outside the house. When you are dressing a bow window, emphasize the shape of the window rather than disguise it. A curved rod hung with conventional draperies or even a softly curved shade would be a suitable solution. If you use a shade, do not be tempted to add any additional decoration or detail.

However, if you wish to decorate the shade, you should try to be as restrained as possible. Remember that a bow window is an attractive feature in itself and should be on display, rather than obscured beneath the ruffles of an overdressed shade.

Furthermore, a bow window and the space beneath it should always be regarded as part of the room in order to create a unified effect. This means that, as long as you have sufficient space available, you can install a seat or even a set of low, curved bookshelves that follow the line of the window.

LEFT *A deep, wide bay window is given a blurred quality through the use of diaphanous sheer fabric that obscures the otherwise rather harsh lines of the window. The combination of sheer curtains and shades also helps to break up the uniform size of the window panes.*

BELOW *Here, separate Roman shades are used for each section of a supersized bow window. The semitransparent fabric and the clean lines of the window give a strong contemporary look to the treatment, which could not be achieved with the amount of fabric necessary to make a series of curtains.*

Curved Windows

It has to be said that curved windows are just as difficult to dress as they were in the past. One possibility is to dress a window of this type with a deep balloon shade in silk or some other lightweight material, so that the curved edge of the shade echoes the curve of the window above. It is important to keep the fabric light and voluminous on a curved window and eschew ruffles along the bottom; silk, although relatively expensive, is ideal. Other options include an unlined cotton chintz or even a heavy sheer.

Conventional drapery styles can also be used at curved windows. The draperies may be made with a relatively stylized heading, such as pinch or French pleats, which is attached directly to the window frame and follows the curve of the window. The draperies could then be tied back at the point on the window where the curve of the arch turns into

the downward fall of the frame. However, bear in mind that such a design would really work only if the draperies were used as stationary panels and rarely, if ever, untied and allowed to fall. Another simple solution might be to hang the draperies from a very narrow rod, placed at the top of the straight sides of the window, in the style of café curtains, leaving the curved top to rise above, free of constraint.

Alternatively, a cornice board or valance could follow the curve of the window, being set above and beyond the window itself. Depending on the depth of the cornice, you could then hang draperies from a conventional rod beneath. If full draperies are not needed, sheer curtains could also hang from underneath a valance, a style that enhances the feeling of lightness induced by a curved window.

A window with a curved top is also the ideal place to try a swagged design whereby a relatively heavy piece of material is attached to the curve of the window and then caught back asymmetrically while a soft fiberglass curtain falls to the floor from underneath. A curved window can also be dressed attractively with light, louvered shutters, perhaps reaching up only as far as the straight sides of the window, which can be folded back during the day and closed at night.

ABOVE *When curved windows are as pretty as these, fitted with their internal shutters, draperies would be more of a hindrance than a help.*

LEFT *These flowing draperies hang beneath a curved cornice which hides the traverse rod mechanism and follows the shape of the windows.*

CENTER *The solution for this window is to ignore the curve and concentrate on curtaining the window below with delicate sheers.*

FAR LEFT (top) *Carefully designed, fanlike shades add interest to a curved window—an interesting solution to an unusual problem.*

FAR LEFT (bottom) *The curved tops of these windows are dressed with stationary panels, tied back at the point where the doors open.*

Door Draperies

In Victorian times, draperies were often used to frame doors, and door draperies are still used today either to dramatically mark an entrance or simply to combat cold and drafts. In the latter case, fabrics such as velvet or silk are ideal because they are warm.

Door draperies can also correct the proportions of an ugly door. If the door is too small for the wall or there is an unattractive "dead" area between the architrave and the ceiling, a drapery with an interesting heading could be hung above the door. Alternatively, the drapery might be hung from underneath a decorative lambrequin, cut to run down either side of the doorway.

Should you want a door drapery on a drafty outside door, it is, of course, important to ensure that it does not impede the movement of the door. The usual solution is either to hang the drapery on the door itself, rather than on the frame, so that it opens and closes along with the door, or to hang it on a hinged rod that swings back against the wall when not in use.

ABOVE *These informal door draperies on a pole are enhanced by a coordinating shade.*

LEFT *This drapery stacks beyond the doorway when undrawn to allow the door to open with ease.*

ABOVE LEFT *Forming a barrier between the hall and the passage beyond, this drapery has an almost architectural simplicity that works well with the polished stairs and tiled floor.*

ABOVE CENTER *This is a traditional solution for a partially glazed door on which only the simplest of drapery designs will succeed.*

ABOVE RIGHT *The almost surreal design of this panel of cloth, which is hung across the door, transforms an otherwise rather dull area into an interesting, inviting space.*

LEFT *This drapery is simply styled and designed more for effect than any particular purpose, acting as a punctuation mark between rooms.*

RIGHT *An otherwise severe environment is softened by a prettily patterned door drapery.*

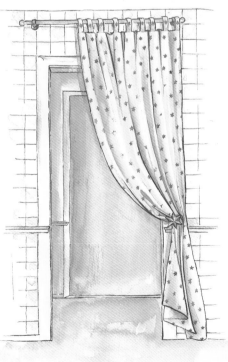

Room Dividers

Draperies make good room dividers, serving a particularly useful purpose when one room has several different functions. In fact, a pair of draperies could be used where a dividing wall has been partially knocked through, leaving a rectangular bridge or arch, especially

if the resulting room looks too long. If the draperies can be seen from both sides, you should use the same fabric for both the curtain and lining, or at least two fabrics that complement each other and suit the room. They do not have to be of a similar weight, especially if the functions that take place in each part of the room are quite different—say

BELOW LEFT *A hall can all too often seem rather open and exposed, but a drapery such as this will keep the area separate without closing it off completely. The drapery is hung to achieve a relaxed, informal effect and is made from a very striking fabric with a large-scale pattern. Draped over a thin metal pole, the colors of this arresting fabric complement the richness of the elegant wooden staircase.*

for dining and sitting or for sleeping and living—but there should be some form of color and design coordination. For example, a warm damask could be paired with a scrunchy silk, while a floral chintz would look excellent with a lightweight striped cotton. These dividing draperies usually look best when secured with tiebacks or brackets, which will enhance the draperies' dramatic effect.

ABOVE, LEFT, CENTER LEFT (top, bottom)
The rich fabric of this drapery adds a distinctive, decorative element both to the hall and to the room beyond. The drapery is further embellished with fringe and braids and reversed to reveal a different, but equally opulent, material. The feeling of luxury the drapery brings to the room is heightened by the tasseled tieback that holds the drapery as well as by the warm color of the wooden floor and the complex pattern of the carpet.

Closet and Alcove Draperies

Draperies and curtains can be used in a host of imaginative ways: instead of glass or wooden doors over cabinets and other storage areas or simply to draw attention to the position of an alcove. One popular style is to thread gathered or pleated curtains onto narrow rods placed inside cabinet doors, behind chicken wire. When choosing a fabric for such a situation, there are some general points to bear in mind. If you are using patterned

RIGHT *The wardrobes lining this dressing room are given a tactile quality with the use of curtains on their doors.*

BELOW LEFT *The easily applied molding from which these draperies hang makes the open closet an integral part of the striped room.*

BOTTOM LEFT *A simple closet is transformed into a glamorous storage space by a drapery that also doubles as a room divider.*

BELOW *A curtained alcove provides privacy and storage space in a room that already contains a bathtub, a bed, and a workstation.*

LEFT, BOTTOM *This all-white bedroom is enhanced by full-length white draperies hung over some open shelves. The draperies have a weighted hem, which helps to keep them firmly and elegantly in position.*

BELOW *A narrow half landing can be turned into a hidden window seat. The alcove is given an air of secrecy with the help of a stunning blue drapery slipped over a pole and held aside with a shaped tieback made of the same material.*

fabric, the size of the pattern is important. It should not, for example, be too large a print or too ill-defined, because when seen through the wire mesh it will look like just a colored blur. Stripes, small geometric prints, or even a solid-colored fabric with some texture would all work well.

Curtains made from a heavy fabric such as felt or velvet, headed in the style of a café curtain and slipped over a narrow rod, can be used to cover shelves in a home office. They are also ideal for covering open shelves in a kitchen or to conceal shelving in a bedroom or dressing room. Although people who rate practicality above decoration might demur,

fabric can also be used to completely disguise ugly heating apparatus such as radiator grilles.

Shades can also be used as an alternative to cupboard doors where space is limited. Pull-down roller or Roman shades over a series of shelves are, in fact, the perfect alternative to a row of built-in cabinets, which might otherwise look like vast expanses of wood and door handles. Many people actually prefer this solution, particularly in a narrow room or passage, because it eliminates the need for enough space to accommodate an open wardrobe door. Roller, Roman, or simply styled balloon shades will keep out dust and give a softer look than wooden doors.

Wall Draperies

It has long been fashionable, particularly in France, to substitute material for wallpaper, with the fabric usually permanently fixed to the walls. However, there is a persuasive argument for using material that can be detached easily, particularly for cleaning or when you are moving. In the past, wall hangings, such as tapestries or pieces of woven silk or wool, provided instant decoration as well as insulation and warmth. Indeed, by the 17th century, they were an important part of

the unified style of decoration that was so admired in England and on the Continent. In rural areas of Europe, the fashion continued for many years. Writing in the mid-19th century, the French novelist Honoré de Balzac describes how, on the feast of Corpus Christi, the wall hangings were taken down and hung outside the windows to decorate the façade and to suggest a festive atmosphere.

Voluptuous draperies, which were pieces of material hung in elaborate swags and then draped over cloth-hung walls, were also a popular fashion in England in the 18th and

19th centuries. The treatment was either pretty or overpowering, the latter often involving heavily draped damask wall hangings embellished with ponderous swags and fringed flounces. Imposing this may have been, but it is also rather excessive and suitable only if you favor a rich look for a dining room or a room used only on special occasions. A different approach, and one that is ideal if you prefer a simpler effect, might be to hang a wall-length drapery underneath a soft, straight valance in a contrasting color.

Other popular methods of decorating the walls include using a feather-light fabric such

OPPOSITE *A heavy, quilted, blanket-weight drapery in a high-ceilinged room serves more than one practical purpose. Not only is it a handsome, textural, decorative addition but it also adds warmth and insulation to what could be a rather chilly room.*

LEFT *Here, a collection of pictures and ornaments takes on a different aspect because of the backdrop of material on the wall.*

BELOW *Hung in loose pleats around the walls, material used in this way has a striking effect that could never be achieved with wallpaper. The color of the wall draperies also complements the throws that neatly cover the sofas.*

in between each point. Alternatively, the fabric can hang from a pole attached by brackets to the wall at either end. There is no need for the fabric to hang from ceiling to floor. In fact, when it is hung halfway or two-thirds of the way up the wall, it may actually serve to correct any flaws in proportion.

When the fabric hung against the walls is of the same design as the window draperies, it can be used to unify a room and give it a softer look. This treatment is quick and comparatively inexpensive to achieve, but it should be done as informally as possible so that the fabric looks as if it is not attached permanently to the walls. This informality is, after all, part of its overall charm.

Material can also be hung along the wall in separate panels or widths in an apronlike style and attached to the top of the wall with brackets or hung from rings on a pole. You can further define the widths of fabric by adding a border of braid or ribbon down each side and along the base. The draperies might be floor length or, in a room with a chain rail, finish level at this point.

as muslin or fine silk hung across a wall to provide a soft and inviting background for the contents of a room. This enticing effect can be employed successfully, for example, behind a bed or sofa set against the length of the wall. The fabric can be attached at various points along the wall so that it drops in shallow loops

In most rooms, the chairs and tables take their cue from the walls, and if you wish to emphasize the look on the walls, you should drape the same material, as long as it is fairly malleable, over selected chairs and sofas. This should be done in an artless fashion so that the fabric looks as if it has just been thrown there informally or simply secured at the back with a knot or a loosely tied bow.

You can also hang any striking length of fabric against a wall by means of decorative, fan-shaped clips fixed to a narrow pole. The fabric can then be moved around at will, as you would a painting. In the same way, an antique shawl may be hung on the wall simply to be admired rather than to serve a purpose.

Depending on what pattern or design of material you choose, hanging wall draperies is

ABOVE *Instant decoration is achieved here with a wall hanging that is easily attached to the picture rail. The advantage of such a wall hanging, which looks so white during the summer, is that it can be exchanged for a warm-colored fabric in colder weather.*

LEFT *Not quite a tapestry, not quite a drapery, this material provides a perfect foil for a collection of art and other decorative objects.*

FAR LEFT (top) *This hall is transformed by covering the wall with a small piece of material that picks up the color of the chair.*

FAR LEFT (bottom) *When these draperies are drawn, the walls and windows of the entire room will look as if they are curtained. Variety is achieved by positioning smaller wall hangings at different points around the room.*

LEFT, FAR LEFT *Here, artfully positioned, tautly stretched wall draperies accentuate the rather inaccessible windows and fulfill a practical role.*

BELOW LEFT *This study corner is made both richer and quieter by hanging panels of thick material in contrasting colors across the wall.*

RIGHT *In an apartment with a dining area rather than a dining room, strips of natural-colored fabric, which are stapled at ceiling level and left to fall nonchalantly on the floor, provide instant drama and amusement.*

BELOW *Perfect for a rented room, these simple wall draperies, tied onto a wooden pole, can hide any number of structural imperfections.*

also one of the quickest and simplest ways of completely changing the style of a room without moving the furniture around. A scrolled and feathered damask, for example, immediately lends a period feel to a room, whereas strong plaids in bold colors or plain panels of fabric in citrus or other lollipoplike colors have a strong, modern look. Similarly, folds and drapes of fabric imply antique charm, while pieces of tautly stretched fabric suggest modernity.

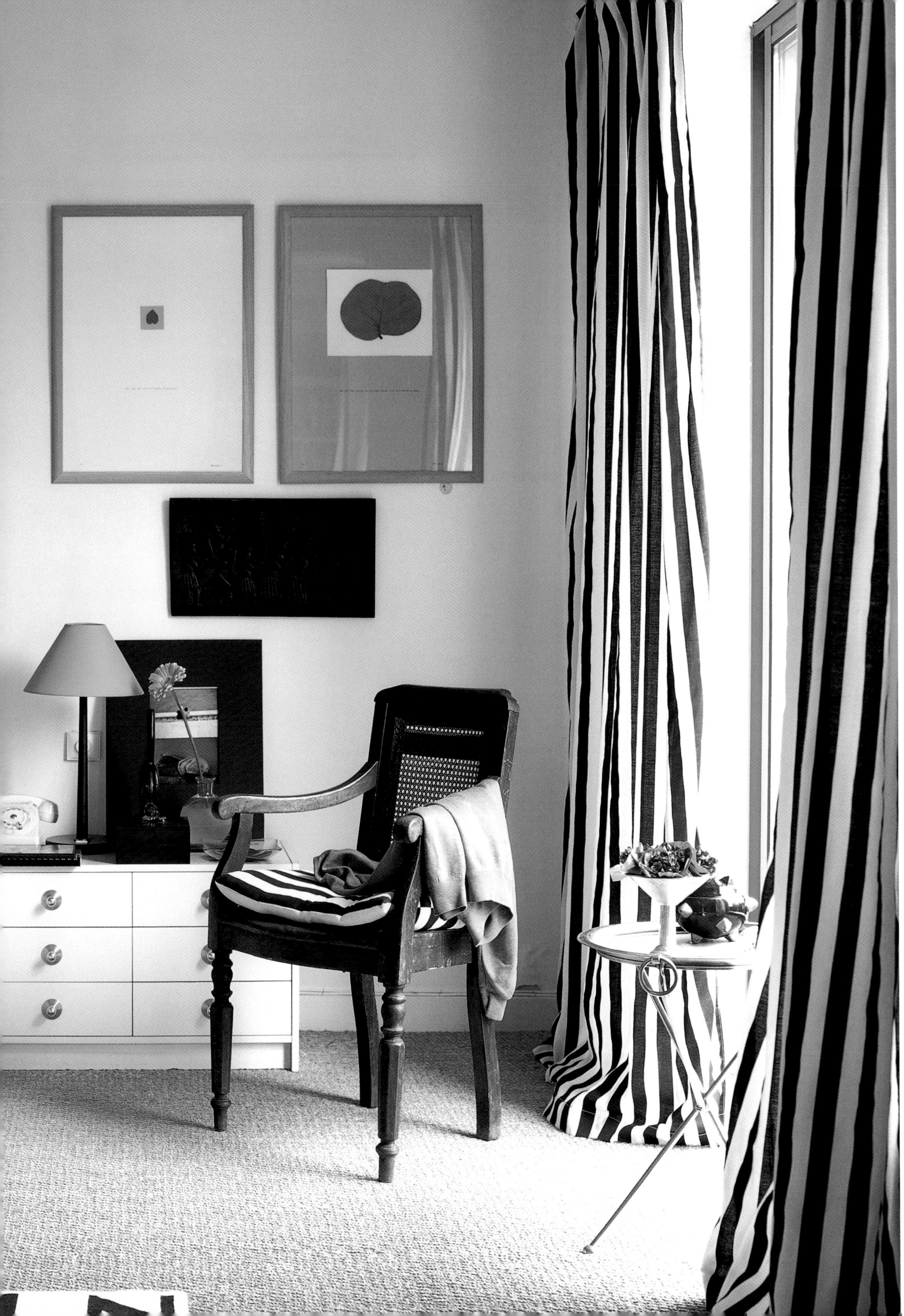

Room Style

ROOM STYLE

Any window treatment should be appropriate to the architecture of the room and the house, and the stronger the architectural presence of a room, the more the draperies or curtains and any other furnishings should reflect that style. Although the draperies are important in themselves, they should also work well with all the other features of the room, from the floor covering to the color and finish of the ceiling. Rooms with different functions also lend themselves to disparate styles of window treatment made in various fabrics with diverse textures. Velvet, for example, has a deep pile and suggests warmth, whereas the geometric slats and reflective surface of plastic or metal Venetian blinds suggest cool efficiency. Many rooms now have several functions, which means that they take on a different air—not necessarily a more informal air, but one appropriate to the activities that take place there. So, the furniture, decoration, and furnishings of such a room should reflect these activities both practically and decoratively. By far the most important consideration when planning a room scheme, however, is that the style should suit you personally, both aesthetically and in terms of how you use the room.

ABOVE *A bedroom window is hung with a Roman shade for insulation beneath a drapery that softens the lines of window and shade.*

LEFT *This window covering exudes as much confidence as the rest of the interior design.*

ABOVE *The eclectic furnishings in this room require a window treatment that is classic in both design and tone. These straight, simple draperies, which flow slightly over the wooden floorboards, provide a dark, striking backdrop for an unusually shaped table and its ornaments.*

ABOVE *Clean, modern lines require equally simple, pared-down draperies. Here, the heading of these unlined draperies made in a plain fabric is concealed behind a wooden cornice board that links the window to other wooden features, such as the paneled door, in the rest of the room.*

Living Rooms

A living room can serve various functions. It may be a formal room, used mainly for entertaining—what used to be called (and in some places still is called) a drawing room. Or it can be the place where the family spends most time when relaxing at home. But whatever you call it, this room has—except in the most formal of situations—a much more relaxed, informal feel than in earlier times, and this should be considered when planning the window treatments.

So, before choosing a style for a living room, it is important to ask yourself when you plan to use the room, for what purposes and activities, and at what times during the day. The answers to these questions should influence the style and type of window treatment you choose.

If your living room is more for the family than for entertaining, then classically formal draperies are not de rigueur, and would probably be inappropriate. If the room is used for combined leisure pursuits, then the decoration, including the draperies, should convey an air of easy relaxation. For example, rich drapery styles made in damask or brocade would look wrong if the rest of the room is furnished in a more utilitarian style. Linen and cotton fabrics, on the other hand, have an air of informality. They are also more practical, being easier to keep clean than more elaborate textiles. This is an important consideration in

RIGHT, TOP LEFT, CENTER LEFT *This living room has a timeless quality and will look as good in fifty years as it does today. Each element is in harmony with the others, including the draperies, which flow naturally from behind the wooden cornice boards. These boards seem to merge into the walls, almost like a continuous cornice.*

LEFT *In another corner of the same living room, the continuous cornice boards are clearly seen running around the perimeter of the walls.*

a room that will probably be used more than any other in the house. Living room draperies should also add warmth in winter and allow in the maximum amount of light in summer. Simplicity is the best approach. You will find designs that are easy to live with include irregular floral patterns, wide stripes, and solid colors in a distinctive weave.

Once all self-respecting drawing rooms had both summer and winter draperies, so that heavier draperies for cold evenings could be replaced with lighter, often flowered, chintzes in the summer. Today, daily life and available time—even available money—do not usually allow for such refinements of taste, but perhaps an argument can be made for

ABOVE, ABOVE LEFT, TOP LEFT *Nothing if not dramatic, these floor-length draperies make a statement of a most definite kind. Caught back to reveal a strongly colored, contrasting lining, they bring even the radiator below into the decorative scheme. The drapery heading is formed into stiffened, handkerchief points that are bound in a contrasting color. Punctuating the junction between the wall and ceiling are two flowers embedded in the heading.*

RIGHT, FAR RIGHT *In this comfortable living room, simple white curtains are rescued from the conventional with bands of contrasting color, one narrow and one broad, the upper band creating the impression of a deep valance. The curtains are attached to the wire with thin, white strips of cord tied to narrow rings.*

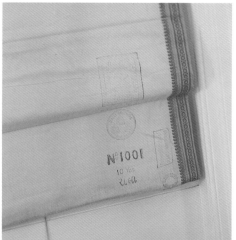

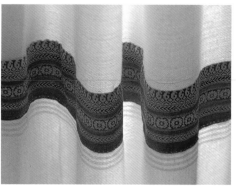

draperies that can be minimized and maximized to provide the same effect. For example, bold panel draperies might be accompanied by a shade, to be used in the winter, with the draperies hanging alone in the summer. Alternatively, panels hung over a self-patterned muslin or other sheer curtain might be removed for the summer, leaving the transparent curtain under a swagged valance.

ABOVE, RIGHT *Comfort is paramount in this living room, in which the windows are unusually tall. The pale curtains are anchored by the band decorative braid set in at chair height.*

TOP RIGHT *Here, the draperies are made from blankets in a striking window treatment.*

CENTER RIGHT, FAR RIGHT *These Roman shades are adorned with decorative red stripes.*

Although both roller shades and, to a certain extent, Venetian blinds were widely used in Victorian drawing rooms, they seem to be less popular today. But they can, in fact, be extremely effective if the room is small but formal. If, however, you prefer a softer look than that given by roller shades or Venetian blinds, Roman shades work well, their rectangular lines, balanced by soft, horizontal pleats, looking just right at single windows. The lines of the shade and the window may be accentuated further by a vertical border.

If the room will be used as a drawing room, the windows should be dressed with style and confidence, and possibly quite grand in concept. Extravagant draperies probably reached a peak of perfection in the 18th and early 19th centuries and can look just as good today if they are tempered with an element of simplicity. This simplicity is the most important aspect of the new thinking in design, affecting almost every part of the decorative scheme. Where possible, however, a drawing room should make some sort of statement, even if the statement consists of something as simple as painting the surrounding window frame in a strong, contrasting color.

Traditionally, formal draperies should follow a certain pattern even when treated fairly simply. They should nearly always be floor length with a striking heading or valance caught or held back in some way. They will not be successful in rooms with the wrong proportions or with very low ceilings, even if the windows would respond to floor-length draperies. When planning formal draperies, you should treat the rest of the room equally formally: hammocks, beaded floor cushions, and ethnic throws should be saved for other rooms in the house. The furniture should also suit the dimensions of the room and be arranged in an orderly way.

FAR LEFT, BOTTOM LEFT Well-proportioned windows can be hung with simple draperies. The wide stripes of color in the floor, furnishings, and draperies provide an air of calm.

LEFT, CENTER LEFT A collector's room, which is full of diverse objects, often has enough to stimulate the eyes of the onlooker. For this reason, the windows are discreetly covered. Here, the Roman shades set within the architrave are functional as well as subtle.

BELOW Deep, plain cornice boards, fixed above the simple draperies, correct the proportions of these narrow but tall windows. The white roller shade beneath both draperies and valance make the window space seem even wider.

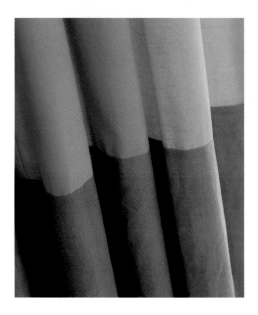

Formal draperies should be full and made in a material chosen for its weight and texture as much as for its design. Damasks, brocades, velvets, and heavy linen all work well, as do chintzes, which should be interlined as well as lined to give them the necessary weight. The choice of pattern should be influenced both by the intended proportions of the draperies and by the height of the room.

BELOW CENTER A shallow bay is dressed with silk draperies that are elegantly overlong, a look that is echoed by the way in which the cloth on the circular table sweeps over the floor.

BELOW, RIGHT When drapery material is as intrinsically beautiful as this heavy, embroidered satin, the draperies are best hung in a simple manner. Here, they are fixed to brass rings threaded over an antique brass pole.

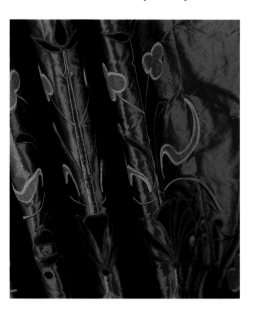

ABOVE, TOP Formal draperies do not have to be beribboned and bowed. These draperies, which are unadorned except for a single row of braid and a shallow but full fringe, convey an air of luxury.

RIGHT These striking stationary panels are attached to the top of a very deep architrave. Tied back at sill level, they give the room symmetry.

Dining Rooms

A dining area may form part of the kitchen or living room or, as in the past, be a separate room devoted solely to entertaining and eating. Obviously, before deciding what style of draperies to have, you should think about what type of dining room you would like.

There is still a need in some households for a formal dining room, in which case the decoration should not be halfhearted. The draperies should make a strong, even dramatic, statement. What is a meal, after all, if not a production? The dramatic style suits almost any shape of dining room and window,

except perhaps a room with a low ceiling and small windows. The effect should, however, be subtle: drama does not mean "over the top" but a bold statement delivered with panache. Such dramatic style could also incorporate an element of surprise, perhaps in the use of color or in unexpected details.

If your dining room is used only at night, window treatments can be even more dramatic, particularly if you prefer to eat by candlelight, which is the most effective and easiest way of setting the dining scene. For example, the draperies might fall in folds on the floor. If you opt for this look, the draperies should be panel draperies and never

ABOVE, RIGHT *Layers of fabric, all harmonizing, build up into a womblike dining room in which pattern is laid over pattern. The valance is echoed by the shape and design of the tablecloths.*

LEFT, TOP *"Rich," "warm," and "inviting" are the words to describe this vibrantly decorated room. Each of the small windows is dressed with a single drapery on a narrow iron pole, tied back with a rope and tassel in the same shade.*

drawn. Artfully arranged, and overlong, such draperies would not have nearly the same artistic appeal if pulled together every night. Alternatively, panel draperies may be joined at the top and caught back with metal or wooden brackets. If the room is used at night, panel draperies are best paired with draw draperies, shutters, or shades.

The color and type of fabric for draperies in a room used only in the evening should be different from those in one used all day long. Colors that would appear "washed out" are not the best choice. Textiles that absorb too much light are not suitable either, although if the fabric has a deep pile, as velvet does, it can add a sense of luxury to the room. On the whole, pale, light-reflecting chintzes do not work as well as bold, strongly patterned ones, while soft, semiopaque fabrics are less effective than well-defined materials.

Whether from choice or necessity, a separate dining room is not an option for many people. Lack of space and a more infor-mal way of life mean that many people prefer to have a dining area within the kitchen or as part of a larger living area. The essential requirements, however, are the same. Colors should be warm and relaxed, the light diffused and soft. Window treatments, including draperies, should be designed to allow in as

much light as possible in the day, yet full enough to provide a cozy feeling at night.

The choice of fabric is as important for informal dining rooms as it is for formal ones. Think carefully before using a floral design unless it is quite structured, because it can clash not only with the food but also with the table setting. Your choice should be neither too bold nor too subtle. Solid colors work well, perhaps with a contrasting border, braid, or fringe around the edges, while geometric designs fight with neither food nor table.

Floor-length Venetian blinds can also be effective, filtering the light and enabling you to create different lighting effects throughout the day. Another option, which is ideal when the room functions as a kitchen and dining room, is to use the same material in both areas but as roller or Roman shades at the kitchen windows and draperies in the dining area.

ABOVE, ABOVE LEFT *In dressing this fascinating room, it would be very difficult to compete with the gothic-style wall hangings. However, the panels, with their black-and-white horizontal stripes, transform the room into an uncompromisingly modern statement.*

TOP, LEFT *A contemporary dining room with flat planes of color is softened by the full, sheer draperies across the windows. Unusually, the traverse rod is not concealed and thus becomes a distinctive feature in its own right.*

FAR LEFT *In this minimalist-style dining room, with its uncommonly wide but shallow windows, roller shades that harmonize with the walls are used to provide a feeling of continuity.*

RIGHT *A breathtaking view of the city skyline requires nothing more complicated than a full drapery in a color that will not detract from the sight of the wonders beyond.*

CENTER *The pole that supports these draperies is suspended from the white beamed ceiling. This makes the ceiling an integral part of the whole drapery treatment. The drapery itself hangs in soft pleats from heavy cords that are attached to the pole, thus breaking up an otherwise rather rectangular composition.*

BELOW, BELOW RIGHT *The impact of this window is maximized by extending the draperies beyond the architrave. The almost imperceptible design of the slightly shimmering material creates a sense of peace and calm.*

LEFT *A simple, unadorned corner used as a dining area is made even more intimate with the addition of a neatly pleated Roman shade. This is both lined and interlined to produce a striking, professional finish.*

BELOW LEFT *A raised dining area and its period furniture take center stage in this uncluttered room. Such a simple interior design statement demands an unobtrusive, almost functional, window treatment.*

BELOW *This elaborate cornice acts as a frame for a wide shade that completely straddles the window in a small dining room. The shade is sewn together in such a clever way that the seams follow the vertical lines of the window frame more or less exactly.*

Kitchens

Over the years the whole concept of the kitchen has changed. Not so long ago, even curtains—let alone full-length draperies—would have been out of keeping with the rather hard, sterilized look of the kitchens of the day. But today, since so many people spend more time in the kitchen, often using it as a living room as well as a dining room, curtains add an air of comfort. Yet, however cozy a kitchen is, remember that it is for the preparation of food. Hygiene and safety are of paramount importance, and since the fabric

used for curtains or shades will get extremely dirty and greasy—which will be clear to anyone who has ever tried to clean the filter of a range hood—you should choose a fabric that can be easily cleaned.

ABOVE, TOP RIGHT *These full-length draperies in a kitchen-cum-living-room are designed so that they do not detract from inevitable kitchen clutter; they run efficiently on a traverse rod.*

RIGHT, CENTER RIGHT, FAR RIGHT *A full-length drapery is combined with a translucent roller shade and adorned with a wide band of fabric that almost reaches the level of the table.*

When deciding on a style of curtain for the kitchen, remember how busy a place it is. In consequence, it is ill-advised to have very elaborate draperies. They would simply look out of place and clash with everything else. Any design you choose should be simple and relatively clean in line. Café curtains, for example, are an ideal choice, allowing you both light and privacy.

Shades or blinds are perfect for the windows above the sink or the drain board. Contained and businesslike, they can look both attractive and welcoming. However, some shades, even if treated, are quite difficult to keep clean. If that bothers you, Venetian blinds in wood, metal, or plastic, which can easily be wiped clean, would make a much better choice for a kitchen.

OPPOSITE *The interest of these draperies, which are hung across the recess rather than against the windows, lies in the material itself rather than in any elaborate style. Attention to detail in the headings of both the curtain beneath the sink and the draperies is more effective than a complicated overall design.*

RIGHT *A wooden shade placed outside eliminates the need for anything more elaborate than simple, unlined curtains, which are made in a blue-and-white checked fabric.*

BELOW, FAR RIGHT *All is not as it seems with this treatment that uses a pair of Roman shades. They are flush with the window, while the decorative headings, which have horizontally striped edges, are slotted onto a wrought-iron pole.*

Bedrooms

Like every other room in the modern home, the bedroom has altered its function—and the way in which it is perceived. It is no longer used just for sleeping but often for watching television or working. But in every day there comes a time when it should be a place of rest, and the window treatment should reflect this.

Not all bedrooms are well proportioned. Indeed, more than any other room, bedrooms are often conjured from strangely shaped spaces such as attics and other areas under the eaves. Unified designs often work best in these badly proportioned rooms, with the same colors and tones used on the walls, windows, and bed to draw attention away from the conflicting angles and corners. Coziness, not

ABOVE, TOP LEFT *An ornate piece of textile is shown at its best when caught up on either side in order to emphasize the central motif. The walls are also decorated with an intricately patterned paper that contributes to the air of wealthy indolence that fills the bedroom.*

ABOVE LEFT *These tieback curtains are slipped over a pole and fastened at the center. A simple shade screens the light.*

grandeur, is the desired effect. Your choice of fabric is also very important: it should provide insulation and keep out the light. Draperies should also be lined and, for maximum heat conservation, interlined. If you choose a lightweight, pale-colored fabric for the draperies, consider using shades underneath, either conventional shades or blackout shades, to reduce the levels of light at night.

Chintz is used in many traditional bedrooms and can look its prettiest and most effective there. English chintzes have been renowned since the 18th century, and in and out of fashion ever since. In fact, the well-known American interior decorator Elsie de Wolfe used chintzes in the early 20th century against a background of quiet disapproval. The best new chintzes are designed with a

ABOVE *Each of the deep windows in this sumptuously decorated bedroom has two pairs of louvered shutters and is curtained along the architrave with single paisley shawls. These shawls are hung by rings from a metal pole. The wall space between the carved architraves is fitted with mirror glass, which unites the windows. The adjacent wall at the head of the bed is decorated with a multicolored plaid covering that enhances the lavish atmosphere.*

In the past, bedroom walls were often furnished with draperies that not only kept the bedroom a little warmer but also unified the overall look. They were either detachable or permanently attached to the walls. If fabric is hung on the bedroom walls, you might like to add an edging along the top and bottom, as well as along the sides, where the walls meet. The best option is to use piping made from the fabric on the walls or, more interestingly, in a color contrasting with that of the wall fabric, perhaps with the same choice of edging for the draperies themselves.

Wall draperies might seem excessive, but it is important to remember that fabrics and

subtlety that makes them potential heirlooms. Recolored and revitalized, these chintzes work very well in both traditional and modern settings. The French equivalent of English chintz is the *toile de Jouy*. These charming, single-color cotton prints are usually set against an off-white background and depict delightful pastoral and village scenes. The complexity of the designs is offset by the relatively simple color range, which is traditionally in various tones of red or blue but often in green, brown, or eggplant purple.

window treatments that would appear flamboyant in another room can look quite at home in a bedroom. For example, silk taffeta in bright colors, figured brocades, lengths of Indian sari fabric, or even Pollyanna-style ginghams all look wonderful in a bedroom. Decorative trimmings can also be used to add interest, so long as they are handled with a light touch. Indeed, multicolored braids and ribbons for edging and tying back will add drama to swags and cascades.

Bedroom windows are also the perfect place to use plain lightweight materials, such as white or cream muslin, figured and embroidered lawn, voile, or silk. Full-length

ABOVE, LEFT *A stiffened valance turns into a deep ruffle that is bordered in deep blue, as are the edges of the checked draperies. The headboard is covered in the same checked fabric to create a harmonious effect.*

ABOVE LEFT, ABOVE CENTER *A loosely curtained wall leads directly to the draperies, which are made of the same fabric as the wall curtains with the addition of a striped border; all the draperies are caught back with a bracket.*

FAR LEFT *Because this bed is placed in front of the window, the draperies are designed to look as much like bed hangings as window draperies.*

RIGHT, BELOW RIGHT *This unusual but highly effective valance treatment is made by using the undulating, wavelike pattern of the fabric horizontally rather than vertically, as on the drapery below. The whole effect is one of neat precision and sophistication.*

BELOW, BOTTOM RIGHT *Here, a false valance, adorned with a thick fringe, is attached to the draperies rather than to the pole above. This is a sensible choice of window treatment for a dark bedroom because it allows maximum levels of light into the room.*

curtains or draperies made from an abundance of sheer fabric can also look extremely luxurious and feminine without being fussy. Sheer fabrics can, of course, be used for glass curtains; or they can also be used as draw draperies over a roller or Roman shade and topped by a valance.

Poles, whether they are made from metal or wood, painted or unpainted, also work well in a bedroom, particularly when they have lightweight finials. They provide decoration without being overbearing. A piece of material draped casually over a pole is always an effective treatment.

ABOVE, TOP LEFT *A bed in the center of the room and a bay window with a view of the garden are emphasized by these classic draperies with their simple pleated heading and border of suitably exotic contrasting fabric. The draperies fall open in an informal, even casual, manner at strategic points around the bay window, which gives the room an intimate atmosphere.*

Bed Furnishings

Bedroom window treatments should not be thought of in isolation. The bed, whether it is covered with a duvet, bedspread, or quilt, is an integral part of the furnishing scheme. This is even more true if it has bed hangings, which have gained in popularity recently. Through-out history the bedroom has been a place of privacy and comfort, as well as a means of demonstrating status, wealth, and power. More money was lavished on the bed

ABOVE, LEFT, RIGHT *This half-tester canopy projects from the wall behind the bed. The drapery against the wall and the pair of lined draperies that hang from the gilded cornice are all made in the same two-toned patterned fabric. The half-tester draperies on either side of the bed are caught back with cords, which hints at the peaceful rest to be achieved when the cords are released. The bed itself requires nothing more than a covering of crisp white sheets and some white linen pillows. In the background, the draperies at the window are simple in comparison with the bed treatment, while the fabric from which they are made matches the underside of the bed canopy.*

hangings than on any other accessories or piece of furniture. Much as they did with window draperies, the Georgians elevated bed hangings and draperies to a fine art, and the Victorians also considered an undraped bed to be bare and unfinished.

You may not like bed hangings, but they certainly add focus to the bed, which is particularly valuable when you consider that modern beds are lower than they were in the past. Dressing the bed can be done in a variety of ways, from the simple to the elaborate. It is

BOTTOM LEFT *In this bedroom, twin beds are transformed with half-testers. Each bed has its own canopy and narrow bed draperies.*

BELOW, RIGHT, BELOW LEFT *This richly bedecked bed is truly a riot of antique textiles. They are used for nearly everything in the bed treatment, including the quilt at the end of the bed. The feather plumes above the canopy are reminiscent of a 17th-century bed of state. The antique textile, which forms the taut canopy above the bed, is also fringed and tasseled. This further accentuates the luxurious atmosphere of the bedroom.*

LEFT *The exposed metal poles of this four-poster bed echo the dark wood of the beams in the ceiling. The thick, cream draperies, which are as simple in construction and style as the poles, are made with a plain tab heading that suits the style of the bed perfectly. When drawn, the draperies surround the whole bed, apart from the area above the bed, which is "open to the sky," and would ensure a quiet, relaxing rest for the occupant.*

BELOW *This freestanding bed has been converted into a four-poster bed by attaching metal columns at each of the corners and running a narrow rod between each post. The wooden heaviness of the bed is admirably offset by the grey, metallic material from which the draperies are made.*

relatively easy to emulate the "state bed" look of the box beds of the past by cutting a cover to fit the size of the bed exactly and allowing it to fall to the floor without pleats or folds. If you have sufficient space, the bed draperies, made in the same fabric, can be headed with a straight valance which is in proportion to the depth of the bedcover. Heavy woven fabrics (those with a pattern that is woven rather than printed), such as tapestry or damask, are the best choice. To achieve the same effect in a small room, the bed could be pushed sideways into an alcove so that the walls create a box. A brass or wooden pole can then run across the alcove to support draw draperies.

LEFT *A bed in an alcove is ideal for a lavish treatment. Here, material is draped in an artless fashion across the alcove, while another drapery hangs behind the bed.*

RIGHT *A strong statement is made with this modern, open four-poster bed in a high-ceilinged room. Full draperies made in a striking fabric are allowed to fall informally to the floor and seem to become part of the design on the walls.*

BELOW *The white-painted beams in this room are echoed by the heavy white poles of the understated bed furnishing scheme. The overall effect is completed by the draperies, left unlined for added simplicity, which hang loosely from the poles.*

In the bedrooms of the 17th and 18th centuries, the bed and window draperies often matched exactly. Even the cornice or valance of a four-poster bed exactly echoed the cornice or valance at the window. Today, this is usually seen as excessively elaborate, except in the most traditional of bedrooms, and, in fact, if the window draperies are particularly complex, very simple bed hangings are the only choice, and vice versa. However, if you decide to hang draperies around the bed, it is important that they reflect the overall scheme of the bedroom in some way. The window and bed draperies do not have to match, but the eye cannot help moving from the bed to the

window and back again. Therefore, it is vital to establish some element of coordination between the two by complementing rather than replicating the treatment at the windows. There should be a link, of course, as there should between any accessories in a room, but it might be in color rather than style, or in the pattern of the fabric rather than *passementerie*.

Toward the end of the 19th century, technical advances introduced tubular metal beds, which replaced wooden bedsteads with their traditionally heavy hangings. Instead of draperies designed to surround the bed, these new metal beds often had rods or narrow poles extending a few feet down from the top of the bed. Suspended from each pole was a small curtain made in a suitably light washable fabric that acted as a screen. Later, the advent of gas central heating eliminated the need for the heavy insulating hangings of earlier times, and for many years thereafter beds remained defiantly unadorned.

The last ten years have seen a new interest in the art and style of bed hangings, although, thankfully, the designs are not quite as complicated as they were in the past. The simplest of all are bed curtains that hang informally from poles fixed to the ceiling.

ABOVE *Hung in the manner of a hot-weather awning, this canopy is simplicity itself. The fabric is attached to a pole on the wall and suspended from another above the bed.*

TOP LEFT *Resembling a giant mosquito net, this airy canopy billows the length of the bed before being caught by a rod fixed to the ceiling.*

ABOVE LEFT *This drapery runs the length of the bed and is caught back at the wall.*

RIGHT *The bed in this relaxing room is given added importance by a simple arrangement of swags hung behind it. A cream drapery hung at the foot of the bed is also inviting.*

They can either fall gracefully to the floor or create a tentlike canopy. Such curtains can be unlined to achieve an even more informal effect. No material is too simple: muslin, cotton sheeting, lining silk, or undyed linen are all suitable. The curtains should be allowed to hang straight down or be tied back with a length of ribbon or braid.

Indeed, airy, almost frivolous, ways of dressing a bed are becoming increasingly fashionable. As in the 18th century, the bed may be set along against the length of the wall and a crown with curved iron rods used as a central point from which to drape curtains above and along the length of the whole bed. Known as a *lit à la polonaise*, it spawned many other fashionable versions. Alternatively, a corona, or crown, might be fixed over the head of the bed and dressed with fabric that drapes abundantly down on either side. Relatively simple to erect, a corona may be either antique or new. They are available in metal and sometimes in wood.

This look is, of course, highly feminine, but avoid confusing femininity with excessive fussiness or frilliness. If you do wish to indulge a liking for ruffles and flounces, either along the edges of the bed draperies or round the valance, make sure that there is enough simplicity in the other elements of the design to balance the frilly touches.

A draped bed does not, of course, have to be feminine. It can be hung with relatively formal draperies and treated in a masculine, almost severe manner. A half-tester or traditional four-poster bed would be more appropriate than any form of corona because rectangular forms are always more masculine than rounded ones. Half canopies were extremely popular during the 19th century and can be easily created today by attaching a false canopy to the wall behind the bed.

Bathrooms

The bathroom has changed in appearance over the last fifty years from a practical, almost utilitarian place to a delightful haven that often sports curtains or shades even if the bathroom window has frosted glass.

Many bathrooms need screening from the outside throughout the day, not just at night, and sheer curtains are ideal for this. They can be full length and cut like heavier curtains, half length like café curtains, or used with more traditional curtains or shutters. An unusual combination is to have one roller

ABOVE, TOP *Since bathroom fixtures and furniture take up so much space, simple curtains that can be easily cleaned are best. These are full and hang from a narrow metal pole attached inside the window frame.*

LEFT *The ultimate plastic curtain surrounds this bath, rather like a cocoon. The black-edged, circular wall mirror behind the bath turns the whole arrangement into a Mondrianesque design. The simplicity of the curtain treatment is ideal for the rather stark whiteness of the bathroom.*

shade made from stiffened material such as voile or gauze, fixed inside the window frame and another, which is only used at night for privacy and insulation, fixed outside it.

For added luxury, you can dress the bathtub. If the tub is against the wall, run a pole along its length and hang a curtain at the end farthest from the taps. For a bath with a shower, a fabric curtain can be used to hide the usually rather ugly plastic inner curtain. If the bathtub is freestanding, attach a corona to the ceiling above the tub and drape a pair of curtains so that they fall, tournament-tent fashion, down either side.

ABOVE *Instead of the customary expandable pole, a fine wire is used to hang these striking black-and-white shower curtains, making them look as if they are suspended in space.*

TOP *The narrow entrance to a shower is made from louvered glass shutters that maximize the available space.*

RIGHT *This "four-poster" bathtub has a freestanding frame from which hangs a pair of curtains. The whole effect is one of witty ingenuity.*

ABOVE *A boudoirlike bathroom with its deep draperies and inner sheers looks very cozy.*

TOP RIGHT *These draperies in a modern bathroom form a backdrop for stainless-steel features.*

CENTER RIGHT *A thick, heavy drapery gives this shower room a voluptuous atmosphere.*

RIGHT *The curtain at this bathroom window is made in a suitably piscatorial fabric.*

Curtains and shades bring warmth and style to a bathroom and a pleasing contrast to the inevitable shiny, reflective surfaces. As in the kitchen, the material used for any bathroom curtains should be lightweight and washable. Condensation, steam, heat, and damp all take their toll on fabrics. Cotton is undoubtedly the best material to use for bathroom curtains as it is easily washed and pleasant to the touch.

ABOVE, TOP *In a small bathroom, a striking and interesting window treatment must combine both practical and decorative virtues. This shade, which is made from strips of fabric woven into a simple lattice, is the perfect choice for a bathroom, allowing in sufficient light if raised while also guaranteeing a good degree of privacy whenever necessary.*

LEFT *Stretched tautly across the window, a printed sheer seems to float above the bath.*

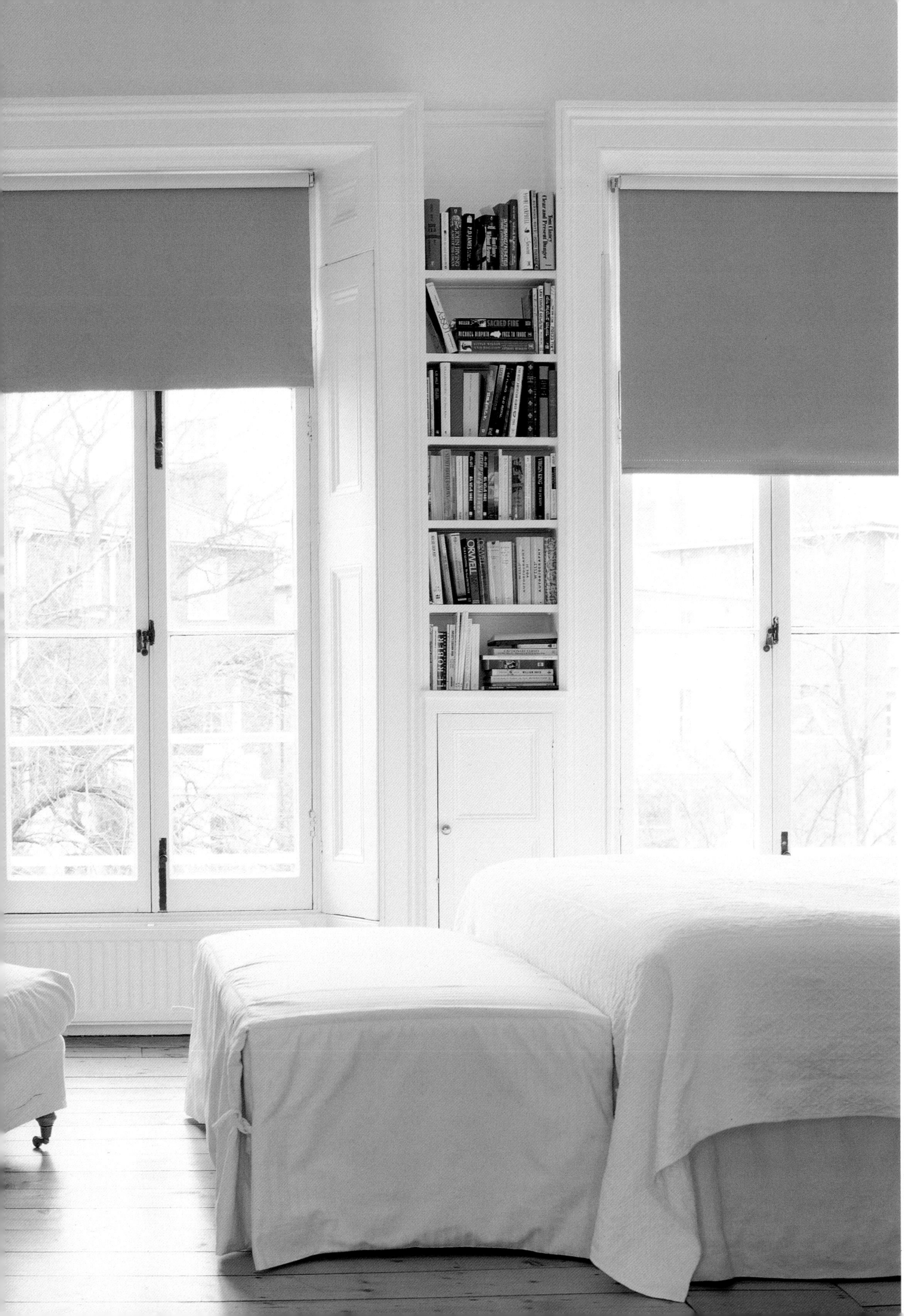

Shades, Blinds, and Sheers

SHADES, BLINDS, AND SHEERS

Shades and blinds play an important role in window design, excluding light and drafts when used with panel draperies or fiberglass curtains, as well as highlighting and completing a window treatment. Used alone at a window, a roller or Roman shade or a Venetian blind suggests a certain streamlined modernity. Shades come into their own in rooms such as the bathroom and kitchen or at windows where the amount of fabric needed for curtains would be impractical. Shades and blinds can also be used in other practical ways around the house, to conceal storage space where doors would be cumbersome or as informal room dividers.

The idea of a curtain or drapery that admits the light is hardly new, and sheer curtains of one description or another have been popular at various times for at least two hundred years. Today, in terms of fiber, finish, weight, color, and design, the choice of sheer fabrics is endless. There is a perfect sheer curtain for every purpose and situation, and lightweight see-through curtains are a useful decorative alternative to shades or draperies where light needs to be diffused or privacy maintained.

TOP LEFT *Here, sheer draperies play a dual role, covering the window and, used across the wall, also giving an illusion of greater space.*

CENTER LEFT *This coarse-meshed fabric is attached to the window frame and secured with a rod in order to serve as a permanent screen.*

LEFT *Split-cane blinds are adaptable and can be made in varying sizes to cover awkward windows. In this room, they are also used over the skylight.*

RIGHT *Wooden louvered windows, the slats of which can be adjusted, allow for privacy in an informal room that also has angled windows.*

Roller Shades

Whereas most Roman shade material can be used unstiffened, the fabrics for roller shades should be chosen with special care. Many will need stiffening so that they can move easily around the roller. Although this process is not suitable for some fabrics, there has been much progress in stiffening techniques, and even some sheer fabrics and laces can be given enough body to hang successfully. Roller shades can be used to correct flaws in window proportion. For example, where there is a large expanse of glass, such as in very wide windows or in deep bays, a series of roller shades will break up the glazed area.

A word of caution is required if you plan to use a roller shade at a small window. The mechanical parts of a roller shade, namely the roller and the two end plates, require that the fabric start some way in from the ends of the roller. This means that you could have a light-revealing gap between the shade and the window frame. However, in rooms with

LEFT *These glass walls are dramatically treated with two very large roller shades set at different levels around the windows.*

BELOW LEFT *This translucent white roller shade makes a decorative statement behind a low bench.*

BOTTOM LEFT *Oversized roller shades are used here to cover a sliding glass door.*

BELOW *To avoid hiding the headboard, these roller shades can simply be pulled up and secured by a system of pulleys.*

FAR LEFT *The glass doors in this bathroom have folding shutters that reach only halfway up the door. Left unpainted, the natural color of the wood blends beautifully with the full-length shade made from split cane. Combining shutters and a shade in this way makes for a feeling of security and privacy.*

LEFT, BELOW *Shades do not have to be made of conventional materials. In this timber-walled room, the shade is made from a rough, hemplike material. This not only allows the light to diffuse through the shade in an attractive manner but also ensures that the shade is strong enough to avoid unraveling. The edge of the shade is bound with a strip of white fabric that further reinforces the shade. The shade can be raised with a simple central cord and pulley.*

sloping windows, roller shades are often the only answer, since they can be fixed at the bottom of the window so that the shade does not flap around when it is pulled down.

The choice of fabric for a roller shade needs careful consideration. Plain, striped, or plaid fabrics are more effective than those with abstract or floral patterns, which are likely to detract from the vertical lines of the shade. If you use a floral or figurative pattern, it is a good idea to anchor the shade visually by edging it with a border that picks out one of the colors in the design. The base of the shade could also be shaped to give it added interest.

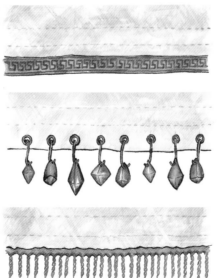

ABOVE *These translucent, rather insignificant roller shades are set close to the windows to emphasize the classic proportions of the room.*

LEFT *A plain, ready-made shade can look both original and personal with the addition of a colorful border or edging. Here, from top to bottom: a piece of braid decorated with a Greek key design is sewn along the bottom of the shade; brass grommets are used to hook on multicolored chandelier droplets that catch the light as they twirl; and some* passementerie, *in the form of fringing and gimp, is applied to the bottom of the shade. All these decorative trimmings can be used to complement and reflect other accessories throughout the room.*

Roman Shades

Roman shades look more sophisticated, and often more formal, than the average roller shade. Although not seen in the past as often as balloon shades (presumably because they were not considered appropriate for grand windows), they were popular in England in the 18th century and earlier. They consist of a flat piece of fabric that pulls up into a series of wide pleats and, when let down, lies flat against the window. Roman shades look very striking set inside the window frame so that the surrounding architrave is exposed. Conversely, on a window that has shutters set into the casing, a Roman shade hung from the architrave allows both window frame and shutters to be seen when desired and gives extra insulation on cold winter evenings. It can also be used to soften the lines of a shuttered window.

The fabric used for making Roman shades does not usually need stiffening, although if they are hung in a bedroom or some other room where light needs to be excluded, it is important to line them just as you would draperies. This does not, of course, apply to a Roman shade made from sheer material, which is a sophisticated answer to diffusing light in a contemporary room in which long draperies would look inappropriate.

Roman shades not only emphasize the vertical plane of tall, narrow windows but can also provide a solution to the often difficult

BELOW LEFT, BOTTOM *A room furnished in such a modest, classic style, with its collection of simple furniture and other soft furnishings, requires only the simplest of shapes at the window. Here, a Roman shade made in a rich, warm yellow fabric needs only the addition of triangular, handkerchieflike points as a decorative finishing touch along the bottom. This serves to complete the ordered symmetry that characterizes the rest of the living room.*

RIGHT, BELOW *This Roman shade is an especially good example of an updated traditional window treatment. Although the design of the material is classic, and the passementerie edging is even more so, the total effect is one of clean modernity. This effect is enhanced by the lines of the architrave which act as a handsome frame for this natural-looking textile picture.*

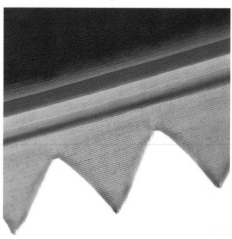

problem of dealing with a window that is curved at the top. Instead of being cut into a rectangle, the fabric can be shaped around a piece of board cut to fit the curve of the window.

Compared to curtains, Roman shades are fairly minimal in concept. A successful way to give them added character is to hang them from beneath a wooden cornice board. Shaped cornice boards, which are easily made with an electric jigsaw or coping saw, can be curved or shaped into ogees, arches, zigzags, or scallops. The board is then covered with material—contrasting with that of the shade—or painted in a solid color and decorated with cutouts such as gold or silver stars, suns and moons, brass escutcheons, or other decorative trimmings. Another option is to decorate the board with a paper border; these are available in sheets from specialist suppliers.

Roman shades are fuller than roller shades and as a result look good at bay windows, particularly if they are set at different levels across the window. Indeed, as are roller shades, they are suitable for large windows and those that are composed of several panes.

LEFT, ABOVE *Within the usual parameters of their basic style, Roman shades can be designed to look more or less formal, according to the surroundings for which they are made. The large window in this very comfortable living room is hung with a Roman shade with shallow, horizontal pleats that draw up into what is almost a deep border.*

RIGHT, TOP *This large Roman shade is made from blue-gray silk—a particularly suitable choice of fabric, because the delicate texture of the material can be clearly seen when the light filters through it, bringing a calming atmosphere to the room. Using such a rich, luxurious material is also an ideal way of embellishing what is essentially a rather simple window treatment.*

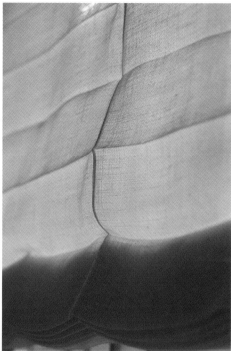

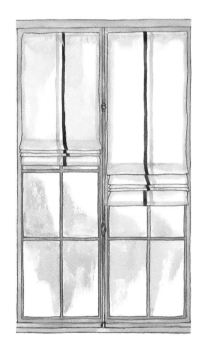

ABOVE *A pair of casement windows is dressed with two narrow Roman shades, the height of which is accentuated by the strong vertical lines of the fabric design.*

LEFT, TOP *When loose, woven fabrics are used for Roman shades, the result is obviously not as crisp as that achieved with a tight weave, but the loose pleats and the fold marks have an informal charm of their own.*

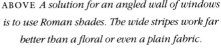

ABOVE *A solution for an angled wall of windows is to use Roman shades. The wide stripes work far better than a floral or even a plain fabric.*

TOP *A window seat calls for a treatment that will not get in the way; a neat Roman shade is ideal.*

ABOVE RIGHT *This bedroom in the eaves has a softened version of a Roman shade, caught so that the softened pleats hang at an angle with the room.*

In fact, a row of shades made in a striking fabric will improve the visual impact of an overdominant expanse of glass. The effect might be accentuated further by making the shades in different widths and setting them at different heights across the window.

Like draperies, shades can be lined to cut out the light or for added stiffness. If, on the other hand, the shade is unlined the light

shining through will give a slightly translucent look to the fabric and create a very pretty effect. Roman shades—or any type of shade, for that matter—are ideal for inaccessible windows. For example, if the window is set at an angle or follows the slope of a ceiling, shades made from a lightweight fabric and drawn over the window can be effective. The window will need an anchor point at the

ABOVE *These loosely pleated shades are caught with a decorative center cord, so that the pleats fan down on each side. The different shades of cord are especially attractive.*

LEFT, TOP *With a simple Roman shade as a backdrop, the deep window sill of this paneled room makes a good display shelf. The window is not centrally placed, so a single-panel drapery on an iron pole is set some way out from the window to improve the proportions of the room.*

LEFT *The glazed doors in this light-filled dining room have been treated with shades. The shades are unlined and made from a fabric with an airy delicacy that looks almost hand drawn. The checked border provides a strong contrast to this intricacy. The matching wallpaper adds to the feeling of fresh, outdoor living.*

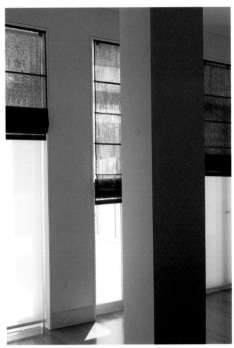

bottom to which the shade can be attached when drawn. They are easy to operate, which will enable you to bathe the room in light during the day and to view the sky at night.

Shades can, of course, be used in conjunction with draperies. Simplicity is the best approach. A neat effect is to edge the shade with a border of the drapery fabric, to unify the two disparate parts; or you might line the draperies in the fabric used for the shade.

ABOVE *A wide, shallow window looks much better with a finely shaped Roman shade than it would with a pair of bulky draperies.*

LEFT, ABOVE LEFT *Windows of different sizes running from floor to ceiling, some of which are obscured by pillars, need to suggest visual unity. These Roman shades, with their abstract design, both unify and add interest to the windows.*

Venetian Blinds

Venetian blinds were originally made from narrow slats of wood and first recorded in the 18th century, when they were known as *jalousies à la persienne*. In their first incarnation, Venetian blinds served the same purpose as slatted or pierced wooden shutters and screens in hot countries, allowing air through but deflecting the fierce heat of the sun. In our own century, the earliest Venetian blinds were made from wide slats of heavy plastic or metal and regarded as a clean, modern alternative to curtains or draperies.

RIGHT *This rather incongruous but effective window treatment combines a minimal white Venetian blind with a cornice board trimmed with traditional decorative fringe.*

BELOW RIGHT *These beautiful French windows, which lead onto the balcony of an apartment, are dressed with Venetian blinds. These blinds are set within the frame of the windows so that when the blinds are let down, they do not impede the mechanism of the door. Left ajar, the windows provide an enticing glimpse of the world outside.*

BELOW *Louvered white wooden shutters are a perfect choice for letting air and light into an open-plan summerhouse.*

Today, Venetian blinds are available in plastic, metal, or wood in a variety of colors as well as with slats in different widths. The slats are linked either with cord or with strips of fabric or webbing, perhaps made in a different color from that of the slats. Indeed, a strong color contrast can transform a blind; for example, contrasting stripes of color on plastic and metal blinds are very effective, whether they are deckchair wide or pinstripe narrow.

Venetian blinds can also be used as room dividers. If they are wooden—whether natural, stained, or painted—they could work well in a sunroom, while narrow-slatted blinds are ideal for bathrooms and kitchens.

ABOVE, TOP LEFT *These white louvered doors are really more like a pair of integral Venetian blinds and provide a useful solution for a window that looks out onto an inner courtyard or garden.*

LEFT, ABOVE LEFT *Wooden Venetian blinds, unpainted and raised by wide burlap tapes, add a feeling of rich warmth and a slightly more natural look to a modern room that has been decorated in a sophisticated manner.*

Sheers

The translucent quality of sheers and the way
they diffuse daylight make them appealing for
any shape of window. They can be used to
good effect on their own or with heavier
fabrics and look particularly dramatic when
paired with a heavily textured wool or damask.
One of the best designers of modern sheers,
Celia Birtwell, sometimes hangs sheer curtains
over, rather than under, a heavier curtain or
drapery. The effect of the opaque material
seen through a translucent fabric adds new
interest to the simplest of window treatments.

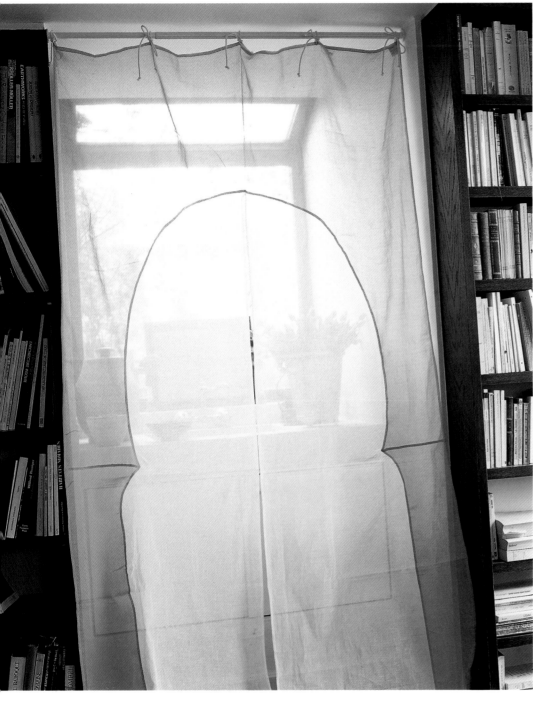

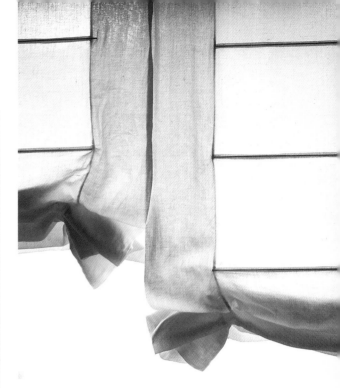

ABOVE, BELOW *These translucent linen shades, resembling large handkerchiefs, have an unstructured feel that counteracts the ordered, geometric design of the room in which they are set.*

LEFT *Like the entrance to a mysterious, exotic tent, this witty sheer curtain screens off a window alcove between a pair of bookcases.*

OPPOSITE (top left) *Dotted with tiny stars, the fragile-appearing fabric of this simple sheer curtain is emphasized by the heavy tasseled metal pole that is used to raise and lower it.*

OPPOSITE (below, top right) *A self-patterned sheer is particularly effective when used like a drapery made from much heavier material. These sheers are caught back beyond the architrave so that the glazed doors can easily be opened.*

There is a range of sheers in different weights and materials, from voile to gauze, often decorated with stars, flowers, and even stylized animals. Such ornamental sheers can be shown off by hanging them in front of a plain roller shade.

Sheers can be the epitome of luxury, and long, muslin curtains hung from a gold pole or underneath a gilded cornice board can look

ABOVE, BOTTOM RIGHT *A wide window is curtained with self-patterned sheers headed with a deep ruffle made in the same fabric. When the curtains are released from the tiebacks, the ruffle has the air of a soft valance.*

TOP RIGHT, CENTER RIGHT *Beneath a cornice board, a double traverse rod holds a continuous sheer drapery and a heavier figured drapery made in a blue-gray fabric. Both draperies can run in unison on the one system.*

RIGHT *In an area that doubles as a living room and an exercise room, the laid-back sheer curtains are attached by extralong strips of material, softening what might otherwise be a rather cold, uninviting environment.*

very luxurious. So, too, can lace curtains, both hand- and machine-made, which are currently enjoying a revival. Panels of antique lace and good reproductions of them can also be found. If you are using antique lace, it is not essential that the panels at the same window match, but if they do not, avoid treating them as an exact pair. Instead, tie them back at different levels, or use one as a curtain and the other as a swag, draped across a pole.

Sheer curtains can also be very practical, being ideal for small windows, where they do not overwhelm. They can also be threaded over a rod at both top and bottom, which is especially useful in a bathroom or kitchen.

RIGHT, CENTER *The appeal of pristine, white curtains is timeless, and there is no necessity to dream up elaborate ways of hanging them. A heading of simple curtain rings, threaded over an old gilded pole, is counterbalanced by a deep hem.*

BELOW *These sheer curtains are not designed to be closed. Caught back to form a design of various angles, they are fixed permanently in position at regular points along the architrave. The angular shapes created by the curtains are echoed by the kitelike lamp shade above the bed.*

ABOVE *Although these sheer curtains could possibly be regarded as rather fussy and elaborate in another setting, the delicate pastel colors of the fabric as well as the intricate delicacy of the pattern are seen at their best when the curtains are hung against the light.*

ABOVE, RIGHT *Hanging antique textiles without harming the fabric is achieved by using some decorative metal clips. These can be attached to traditional curtain rings which are then threaded over a pole in a color that harmonizes with the curtain material.*

DETAILS

Draperies are a vitally important part of the design scheme in a room. They catch the eye immediately and are one of the first features that people comment on. A sofa, for example, has to look really terrible or absolutely wonderful before it is mentioned, but nearly everyone has an opinion on the draperies. Draperies, curtains, and shades can be greatly enhanced by adding decorative details, for it is the details that emphasize the design of the window treatment. The detail may be as simple as a braid, ribbon, binding, or a tassel, or as striking as an ornately carved pole with finials. Each detail you choose must be applied as carefully and neatly as possible, because the effect of the most beautifully made draperies will be ruined by an untidy fringe or a badly sewn tieback. When adding decorative details, do not confuse the idea of fine detail with fussy or fancy additions. The best details within any decorative scheme should simply emphasize the line of the draperies themselves. Not only must the details be beautiful in themselves, they should accentuate the beauty of the window treatment and the room.

TOP LEFT *This piece of material appears artlessly tossed over the top of the drapery, but the treatment is, in fact, carefully thought out. The contrast in textures, the border, and the ribbon detail all draw attention to the window as a whole.*

CENTER LEFT *A window without a curtain is dressed with a valance of long white handkerchief points that contrast with the black rings and pole.*

LEFT *In this shade the broad stripes of the material contrast with the natural weave. The shade is attached to the architrave with neat brass hooks.*

RIGHT *Against the dark wooden frame of this window, the curtain rings are tied with cords to a length of thin wire. Each piece of cord is knotted at the end in an informal manner which complements the simplicity of the curtain.*

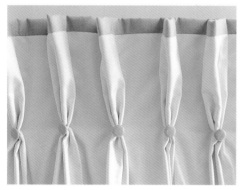

Rods, Poles, and Finials

Headed draperies with no cornice or valance can be hung on poles, but most other types of drapery should be hung from a conventional rod, usually made from either plastic or metal, and concealed behind a valance or cornice. An alternative to a decorative wooden cornice is a narrow piece of board covered in the same material as the draperies. The positioning of the rod when you are hanging your draperies is vital. It is either attached to the top of the architrave or, more probably, secured in the "dead" space between the architrave and the ceiling. It all depends on how elaborate and deep the drapery heading is.

A conventional rod is specifically designed to be functional. Beauty does not enter into the equation. These rods can be bought ready-made or custom-made to fit the dimensions of the window exactly. Cut-to-measure rods are available in curved styles to fit bow windows, or angled to go around corners. Double rods permit you to hang a pair of opaque draperies over sheers. Make sure to buy a good-quality rod, adequate for the weight of your draperies.

TOP LEFT *This drapery is designed for awkward corners and set onto a specially curved rod.*

CENTER LEFT (top) *The contemporary feel of this traditional French-pleated drapery is achieved by colored edging and buttoned pleats.*

CENTER LEFT (bottom) *A smocked heading has a softer, more informal effect than a pleated one.*

LEFT *Widely spaced pinch pleats such as these give an almost casual air and are suitable where there is no space for more elaborate heading styles.*

CENTER RIGHT *A wooden cornice is ornament enough for this simple drapery.*

RIGHT *A simple roller shade is covered by a drapery on a metal rod with decorative details.*

If the draperies are to draw (unlike stationary panels), you will need to use a traverse rod. In addition to conventional traverse rods, decorative styles are available; in these, the cords and sliders are concealed behind a hollow pole. A cheaper alternative, if the draperies are made from lightweight or sheer fabric, is to attach a drawing wand to the top inner corner of each panel. These are then used to open and close the draperies.

Whereas swags and cascades are sometimes seen as feminine, poles and finials have a masculine character and suit tailored draperies

LEFT *An elaborate and beautiful plaster ceiling cornice needs no more than a simple metal pole arrangement below it. The simplicity of the draperies also emphasizes, through contrast, the ornate complexity of the plaster design.*

BOTTOM LEFT *A quilted fabric, which has been trimmed to look as if it is reversed, is suspended from a metal pole by narrow contrasting rings.*

BELOW, BELOW LEFT *A brass pole and grommets, along with ornamental brass brackets, enhance the richness of the patterned fabric and the overall design of this comfortable dining room.*

LEFT *These tieback curtains, permanently fixed at the center, are finished with a casing that runs through a pole with spearheaded finials.*

RIGHT, CENTER RIGHT *These draperies are suspended from a pole fixed just below the ceiling. They are unlined to the depth of the window, so they act somewhat like a sheer and pleasantly diffuse the light.*

BELOW *A peg board made to the same depth as the outer architrave is fixed above the window to provide an unusual support for the long loops of the curtain. The whole effect is simple but effective, reflecting the Shaker style.*

and well-proportioned windows. Decorative rods are available in a variety of sizes, from narrow, brass café rods to thick wooden poles. They are useful, if not essential, when a drapery does not have an elaborate heading. Rods are also smarter than the spring-pressure curtain rods often used for bathroom and kitchen windows.

The most popular materials for both rods and finials are brass, iron, and other metals, as well as wood and resin, which can easily be molded into different designs. This means that finials can be as simple as a ball or as elaborate as a lion's head and mane. Finials are sometimes bought separately, and so it is important that they work well with the pole.

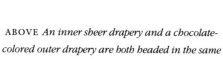

ABOVE *An inner sheer drapery and a chocolate-colored outer drapery are both headed in the same simple way to create a harmonious effect.*

LEFT *Tabs fix these draperies to a pole. A single tassel hangs prominently in the center and throws the draperies into sharp relief.*

RIGHT *These small white curtains, which hang beneath a bathroom sink, are tied with small bows to a thin rod. The intricate, lacelike edge along the bottom of the curtains brings an element of delicacy and femininity into a room that can often seem rather stark and utilitarian.*

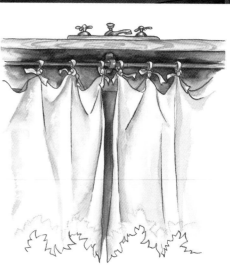

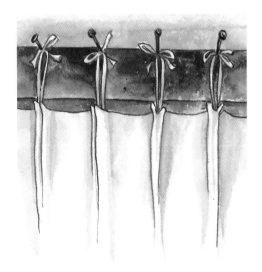

ABOVE *When a curtain is attached to a rod with strips of fabric, the length of the strips can alter the look of the curtains. Here, long strips around a self-colored pole make the curtain seem to float.*

CENTER LEFT *Curtain clips, which are available in various sizes and finishes, give an informal look to any curtain.*

LEFT *Decorative twine secures this curtain to a painted tree branch in a highly original way.*

FAR LEFT *Basic but interesting, this curtain is fixed to the board with bows hanging from nails.*

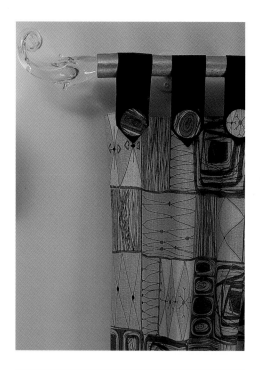

LEFT *This strongly patterned curtain is balanced by a heading of broad tabs, each of which is finished with a fabric-covered button that harmonizes with the main fabric. The pole itself is gilded for extra impact and finished with an elaborate glass finial.*

RIGHT *A traditional wooden pole and rings are brought to life by the addition of a gleaming brass bracket. The rich dark color of the wood provides a beautiful contrast to the pale-colored draperies.*

BELOW LEFT *Wrought-iron rods work very well with brightly patterned fabrics, particularly when they are attached with double-link chains.*

BELOW RIGHT *Antique French finials, brackets, and decorative rings are in strong contrast to the unlined drapery beneath.*

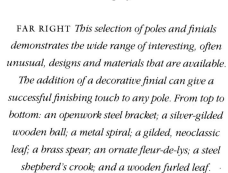

FAR RIGHT *This selection of poles and finials demonstrates the wide range of interesting, often unusual, designs and materials that are available. The addition of a decorative finial can give a successful finishing touch to any pole. From top to bottom: an openwork steel bracket; a silver-gilded wooden ball; a metal spiral; a gilded, neoclassic leaf; a brass spear; an ornate fleur-de-lys; a steel shepherd's crook; and a wooden furled leaf.* ·

BELOW *Finials today range from those styles that were popular in the 17th and 18th centuries to contemporary and even futuristic designs. Finials are made in a variety of materials including metal, wood, plaster, glass, and resin. From left to right: a gilded spearhead; a turned wooden ball; a gilded leaf; a wooden acorn; a steel fleur-de-lys; and a turned, gilded globe.*

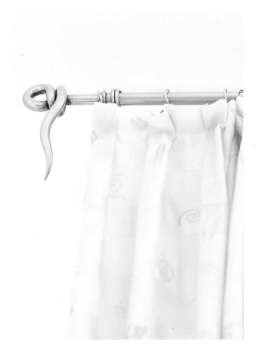

ABOVE *These draperies are finished with material knotted like a scarf, which conceals the bracket.*

ABOVE LEFT *The simplicity of a pole and drapery is offset by the curves of the finials.*

LEFT *An oversized bow in the same material as the draperies softens the brass pole and finials.*

BELOW LEFT *This unusual rod is made by binding many thin multicolored rods together. The intricacy and detail of such a rod eliminates the need for elaborate brackets or finials.*

BELOW *The drapery in this classic room is finished with gilded, spearheaded finials, a mahogany pole, and brass rings.*

143

Swags and Cascades

Many draperies and windows are enhanced by the addition of swags and cascades, but the depth and length of each element of the design should be carefully worked out. The design of both swags and cascades should be fairly simple. A small window, for example, needs no more than one swag and a balancing pair of cascades, whereas up to three swags may be used on larger windows. You should also bear in mind that the more swags on any one window, the more prominent the accompanying cascades should be.

ABOVE *The swags and cascades at each of these windows create an asymmetrical effect.*

TOP LEFT *This traditional window is perfected by a swag and cascades in a gauzelike material, attached within the window frame.*

TOP CENTER, ABOVE RIGHT *A single drapery panel is attached to an iron pole and secured at the side of the window. A striped swag is caught over the pole and falls into an informal cascade.*

RIGHT *These are swags and cascades in the grand manner, with full-length draperies embellished by three swags and cascades. Rosettes hold each swag; the fringe accentuates the design.*

Swags and cascades can very often look effective above a pair of draperies in a different fabric. Rigidly classic swags, perhaps in a heavy silk, look good above sheer draperies at a tall window, while swags and cascades made from pieces of antique material are shown to advantage above plain draperies. If a window lacks any architectural interest, a well-designed arrangement of swags can make it look more inspiring. But whatever design you choose, from traditional swags and cascades to a piece of fabric draped informally over a pole, do not skimp on fabric. Properly made swags involve more material than you might think.

LEFT *This is a witty version of a traditional swag. The deep swag, which is caught in the center and edged with bobbles, hangs over two narrow strips of folded fabric and frames the view beyond.*

BELOW LEFT *Double swags are divided by a central cascade and held at the sides by rosettes.*

BOTTOM LEFT *The use of a luxurious yellow fabric is justified for such a formal arrangement.*

BELOW *An elaborate arrangement of swags and cascades involves one swath of material caught at a center point on the molding. A contrasting fabric is looped across it and falls in cascades on each side. A shade is all that is needed below.*

Valances and Cornices

One of the glories of 18th-century windows in grand houses were the wooden or plaster cornices, which were ornately carved and gilded. Like the crown of a picture frame, they straddled the window confidently, while from beneath them hung equally confident draperies or balloon shades. At the other end of the scale from these rather grand cornices were shades and simple draperies hung from behind a flat board made from wood that was either left unadorned or decorated with exquisite images of flowers and fruit on a painted background.

Although window treatments today are generally lighter in appearance, there are many situations in which draperies look far better with a valance or cornice, rather than just a heading. A valance or cornice is a defining and anchoring device and can give added importance to a window. However, the look of many windows is ruined by a top treatment that is out of proportion with the draperies below. Small windows with short curtains or

draperies, for example, require no more than an apronfrill, while tall windows need a deep and relatively imposing valance of some distinction. A rough guide is that the valance should measure about one-sixth of the finished drapery length. Although this is a generalization, it provides a useful starting point for ideas. Valances can even be used on their own without a pair of draperies below or perhaps just with a plain shade to give definition to windows that would be overwhelmed by draperies.

Today, a gilded and carved cornice would cost a great deal to have made, although there

ABOVE *Here, an ornate valance follows the lines of a bay window. The shape of the window is further accentuated by the diamond-shaped panels that run along the edge of the valance.*

ABOVE LEFT *This stiffened valance is composed of curved panels, each of which repeats and draws attention to the motif on the draperies.*

RIGHT *Light, gauzelike draperies are held back with ropes that are attached to brackets on the architrave. The draperies are topped with a loose decorative swag in a richly colored fabric that is draped neatly over a heavy gilded pole. The color of the swag is identical to that of the rope, for a unified effect.*

FAR RIGHT *Rather unremarkable full, unlined draperies are brought to life with a stiffened valance that dips down in a sweeping curve.*

are still certainly many craftsmen skilled enough to make them. An easier option is to use a decorated wooden or resin cornice, which is cut to fit the width of the window, and shaped to suit the draperies. The panels can then be painted and decorated with appropriate motifs. You should be able to find a specialist designer who makes different styles of cornice, many of which are copied from original designs. It is not, of course, difficult to make cornices at home. The board could be cut into different shapes, whether scallops, squares, fans, or triangular points, either by penciling the shape you want directly onto the board and then cutting out the design with an electric saw or by making a paper template first. You could then decorate the board in any number of ways. For example, it might be painted, stenciled, papered, or even decorated with colored tapes, ribbons, or motifs from a child's scrapbook.

A wooden cornice—whether straight or shaped—can also be covered with the fabric used for the draperies. However, if you use a

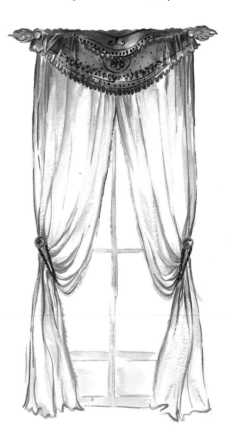

earlier times a shaped—or flat— valance was often hung from beneath a wooden cornice, which might be carved and even gilded. Such complicated arrangements are rarely used today; however, a shaped valance can be very grand in itself. The valance is usually stiffened, with interfacing and/or interlining, and finished with a lining. As on a cornice, the lower edge may be shaped in whatever style seems appropriate to the treatment. It may also be trimmed with braid, piping, or fringe.

A softer, more informal option than a cornice or shaped valance is a pleated valance. This is normally hung from a curtain rod placed in front of the draperies—although it may instead hang from a valance shelf—and is pleated in the same style as used for them. If used with lined draperies, the valance should also be lined.

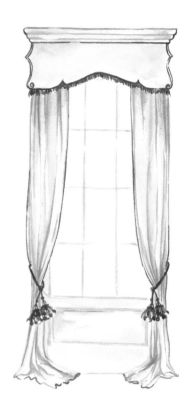

contrasting fabric, the general rule is to balance a geometric with a floral, or a solid, design in colors that complement each other. It takes a very experienced eye to use one stripe for the draperies, for example, with a completely different stripe for the cornice. Another treatment is to use the drapery fabric for the cornice but in a different way. For example, the central motif might be cut out and appliquéd onto a solid-colored back-ground; or, with a geometric design of stripes, zigzags, or diamonds, the fabric could be cut out so that the pattern lies horizontally.

In contrast to a cornice, a valance is made entirely of fabric, although it is often hung from a piece of wood, called a valance shelf. In

RIGHT, ABOVE *The impact of this bay window is strengthened with a bold valance. The oversized design of the urns is used with an equally strong, striped fabric to emphasize each angle of the bay.*

ABOVE RIGHT *Delicate unlined draperies fall from a molded cornice and deeply shaped valance. They are edged in the same color as the fringe on the valance and the tassels of the tiebacks.*

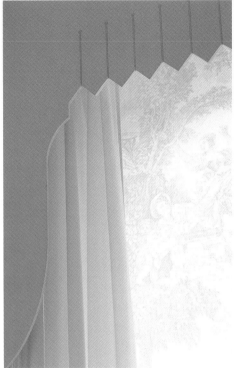

ABOVE *This valance is cut into different lengths, so that the vertical stripes act somewhat like a fringe while the draperies are edged with stripes.*

LEFT, TOP *A wooden cornice board hangs over a pair of draperies. The effect is subtle, rather than overdone, because the cornice board is the same color as the drapery fabric.*

In addition to such classic top treatments, many other effects are seen today. A piece of fabric may be casually draped over a rod, for example. Often this approach is used to show off an antique or handmade textile, which provides a striking contrast to the draperies. The textile may even have a hole or two—which will, of course, make it less expensive. An old silk or paisley shawl can be draped into a swag to suggest antique richness.

ABOVE, ABOVE LEFT *Narrow strips of natural-looking cloth, simply but beautifully embroidered, are fashioned into a pleasing pair of draperies and a valance. The combination of a gently undulating valance and a pair of straight-edged draperies is visually striking.*

TOP LEFT, TOP *From a molded cornice, designed to follow the corners of the walls, a deep border of antique woven tapestry is edged with a fringe of tassels to become an ornate valance.*

LEFT, TOP, ABOVE *A small, rather insignificant window is given new importance with the addition of a deep lambrequin that extends to the edge of the architrave and then curves downward. This alters the dimensions of the window below, making it more interesting and striking. The braid and fringe on the lambrequin is also echoed in the unusual narrow, handmade lace shades set at different levels across the window. The delicacy of the shades contrasts markedly with the heavier lambrequin.*

151

Tiebacks and Brackets

By the 18th century, draperies were usually either caught back with an ornate confection of braids and tassels or restrained with fittings such as brackets, which had a more architectural quality. Both brackets and tie-backs are used extensively in window treatments today, and this is understandable.

You will find that antique brackets are rather expensive but, on the other hand, do hold their value. For a comparatively small outlay, they not only serve a practical and decorative purpose but can instantly alter the look of the draperies. A ready-made, overlong

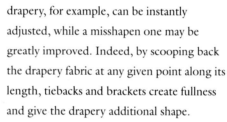

drapery, for example, can be instantly adjusted, while a misshapen one may be greatly improved. Indeed, by scooping back the drapery fabric at any given point along its length, tiebacks and brackets create fullness and give the drapery additional shape.

In practical terms, they also allow as much light as possible into the room. In decorative terms, there is no limit to the uses for tiebacks and brackets, serving as they do to alter and pull together the look of both the curtains and the whole room. However, more importantly than for any other type of drapery accessory, you can correct the proportions of the drapery by carefully positioning a tieback or bracket.

Tiebacks and brackets can be either spartanly simple or dauntingly elaborate. The first design rule when deciding what to marry with a pair of draperies is to choose opposites: pair elaborate trimmings with simple draperies and vice versa. All too often draperies that are already overdesigned are burdened down with the weight of gilded tassels, braids, and other tiebacks, scooping the folds of fabric into heavy curves and loops. By all means add an eye-catching tieback such as an oversized tassel or a heavily gilded rosette, but use it with a simply designed drapery, perhaps in a

ABOVE *A fabric tieback made in one of the colors of the drapery is padded to give it impact.*

ABOVE LEFT *A door drapery, bordered with a geometric design, is tied back with a band to which rows of small shells are fixed.*

TOP *When a traditional rope-and-tassel tieback is used, it is important that it be heavy and thick enough for the weight of the drapery.*

LEFT *In this period room, the drapery, which is longer than floor length, is held back by a cord embellished with a double tassel.*

material that is solid colored or has a self-striped pattern. Although using a heavy tieback with a drapery in a correspondingly heavy material can be successful, there is also an argument for using a weighty tieback with a fragile fabric, such as unlined silk, to create a dramatic contrast in both texture and weight. Single drapery panels can also benefit from the judicious use of a tieback, particularly when there is a sheer curtain or shade underneath.

Tiebacks were formerly often made from the same material as the draperies, although this approach now seems somewhat dated. They were either left unstiffened or shaped around a template, often in a curved or

scalloped shape. Another popular idea was to complete the tieback with a rosette of fabric, either in the drapery material or perhaps in a contrasting fabric. Rosettes were, in fact, used extensively in 18th- and 19th-century drapery design and can be very effective, although

ABOVE, RIGHT *All the elements in this window treatment are in the same shades of tobacco-brown. The inner and outer draperies are both held back by the same double corded and tasseled tieback. Such similarities mean that the overall effect in this rather sophisticated library is sumptuous but soothing.*

they must be sufficiently generous and look more like a full-blown rose than a never-to-open bud. The tradition of *passementerie* has also given us cord or rope tiebacks that are often decorated with tassels. Plain or tasseled, they will look equally good on the right draperies. Like all tiebacks, they can either be secured to a hook fastened to the architrave or simply tied round the drapery itself.

Of course, there is no reason why you should have a traditional tieback or bracket in any case. With a lightweight drapery, a wide ribbon simply tied in a bow can look very striking, as can a hank of raffia on a pair of draperies at French windows that lead into the garden. A natural-looking fabric can even be tied back using some thick, rough twine or unbleached rope. Also, if you are bordering a solid-colored drapery with braid, cord, or fringe, a simple tieback made from the same material as the border would create a strongly unified effect at the window.

In the past, brackets were very popular drapery accessories. They were either curved and cast in a metal such as brass—gilded ormolu for expensive draperies—or sometimes even carved in wood. Nowadays, brackets are usually made in either metal or wood, and

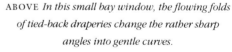

ABOVE *In this small bay window, the flowing folds of tied-back draperies change the rather sharp angles into gentle curves.*

ABOVE LEFT *A flat band of material is simply but effectively embellished with a rosette made from the same material.*

LEFT *Braided cord makes one of the simplest of tiebacks and works best when used with a drapery made of fabric with a different texture.*

FAR LEFT *The visual interest here comes from the strong contrast in texture between the heavy rope tieback and the delicate unlined drapery through which the light shines.*

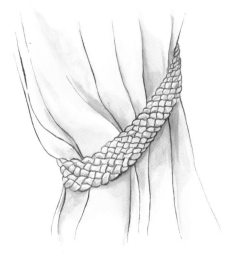

ABOVE *The coils of this rope blend with the stripes of the drapery in a particularly soothing way.*

ABOVE LEFT *A thickly textured tieback holds this heavy plain drapery in place.*

LEFT *This centered drapery has a tieback in the same material, which is smocked somewhat like the sash on a child's party dress.*

BELOW LEFT *A band of simply embroidered fabric makes a charming tieback.*

BELOW *A tieback in the same fabric as the drapery avoids detracting attention from the lines of the drapery itself.*

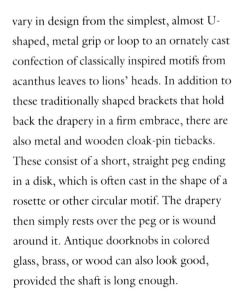

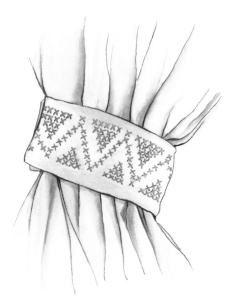

vary in design from the simplest, almost U-shaped, metal grip or loop to an ornately cast confection of classically inspired motifs from acanthus leaves to lions' heads. In addition to these traditionally shaped brackets that hold back the drapery in a firm embrace, there are also metal and wooden cloak-pin tiebacks. These consist of a short, straight peg ending in a disk, which is often cast in the shape of a rosette or other circular motif. The drapery then simply rests over the peg or is wound around it. Antique doorknobs in colored glass, brass, or wood can also look good, provided the shaft is long enough.

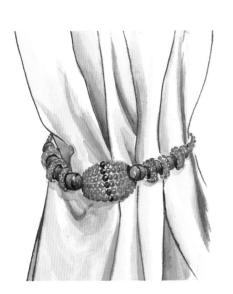

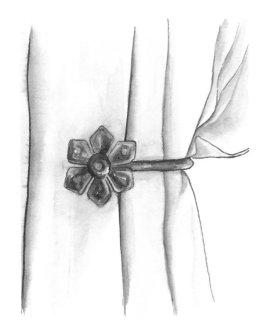

OPPOSITE (far left) *The iron pole is echoed by the curved iron tieback on these three-quarter-length curtains.*

OPPOSITE (top) *Easy to use and extremely effective, lengths of chain are wound neatly around the drapery in a traditional tieback fashion.*

OPPOSITE (center) *Often used in the 18th and 19th centuries, these decorative round-headed pegs allow the drapery to be looped luxuriously over them.*

OPPOSITE (bottom) *The elegant curve of this horseshoe-shaped bracket, with its decorative finial, catches the light.*

ABOVE *A modern variation on a theme, this striking metal-and-glass bracket is ideal for a strongly designed contemporary fabric.*

TOP LEFT *A three-dimensional tieback can be made with a bright ethnic necklace or, alternatively, with individual beads threaded into an appropriate design.*

ABOVE LEFT *Draperies made from a fabric that is as rich and luxurious as this look so much better when they are held back with a gilded peg rather than a tieback.*

LEFT *A fixed decorative bracket allows for more precision in the draping of the material than a fabric or cord tieback.*

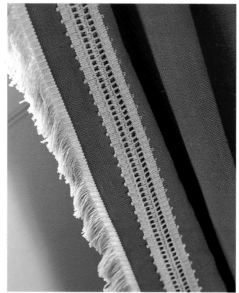

Decorative Trimmings

Well-made trimmings, or *passementerie*, such as braid, fringe, gimp, woven borders, bobbles, and ruffles, may seem expensive at first but are definitely worth the investment. Working braid or gimp into coherent designs in many colors or making a weighty tassel is a lengthy and complicated business. As usual, a sense of proportion is very important. A charming little bobble or piece of braid seen in a pattern book should be envisaged on a whole valance or swag or running around the edge of a drapery. Will it be dwarfed, or, conversely, will it overwhelm the drapery?

There is a wide choice of trimmings available, usually made from cotton, silk, or wool and combine varying colors and woven effects. Faced with such a selection, it is all too easy to regard trimmings as an instant salvation for a rather dull pair of draperies, and be tempted to choose everything. But this is an occasion when the maxim "less is more" holds true. Pin a sample of your chosen trimming onto the drapery fabric to see whether the draperies and the trimming work effectively together. In short, trimmings should contrast with and complement the drapery, defining its lines.

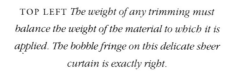

TOP LEFT *The weight of any trimming must balance the weight of the material to which it is applied. The bobble fringe on this delicate sheer curtain is exactly right.*

ABOVE, TOP CENTER, TOP RIGHT *Although fringe can be made to any length, it is important to match the length to the design of the drapery.*

ABOVE RIGHT *Fine pieces of embroidered textile such as this can be enhanced by the right choice of trimming.*

RIGHT *Two rows of crimson braid as well as a tasseled fringe are not too strong for intrinsically plain draperies.*

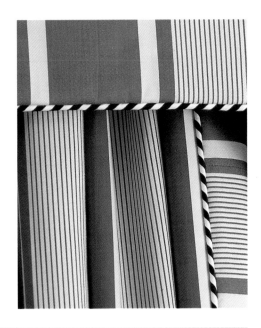

FAR LEFT (top) *This sophisticated border has the same striped theme as the material of the drapery and valance, only in miniature.*

LEFT *This border is highly successful because it complements, rather than contrasts with, the softly hued draperies.*

FAR LEFT (bottom), BOTTOM LEFT *This drapery is embellished solely with a band of braid.*

BELOW LEFT *On a Roman shade, a bobble fringe, dyed in the same color as the stripe, adds interest when the shade is raised.*

BELOW *Here, the fabric is cut to make a border shaped into a loose decorative scallop.*

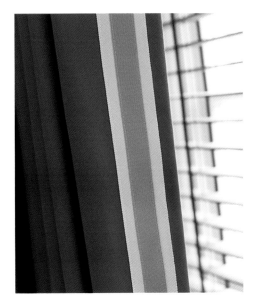

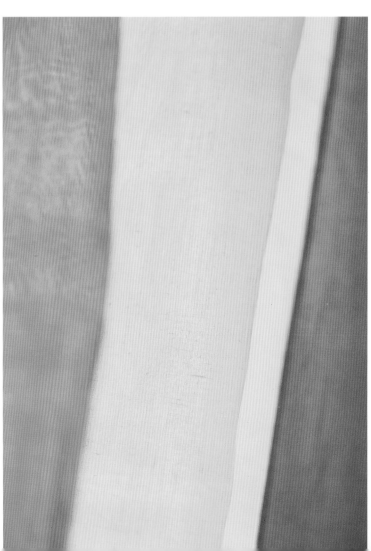

PRACTICALITIES

You may find that you need to make your own draperies, curtains, or shades because you have just moved into a new home; or you may simply enjoy designing your own window treatments. Whatever the reason, one of the most important considerations before embarking on any sewing project is to plan thoroughly what you intend to do in order to achieve the best results. For example, you should consider where you are going to work and what worktable or other surface you can work on, as well as decide on the best type of fabric to use and whether you will also need lining fabric. With careful measuring and cutting out, your home decorating projects should all run smoothly and successfully. This section outlines the basics of drapery and curtain making; clear instructions on stitches, seams, and other sewing methods are given in "Sewing Techniques," on pages 179–181.

MEASURING

This is the most important stage when making window treatments and should be considered carefully. The fabric quantity depends on the style of drapery or curtain, so you will have to decide whether you want them to be full length, over-sill length, or sill length (as the vertical arrows below indicate) and take accurate measurements. Curtains often hang inside the window recess, draperies generally outside it (as the horizontal arrows show). Other factors to consider include the heading style, the fullness of fabric, and any pattern repeat.

Heading Styles

When choosing a style of heading, you will have to consider the size of window, the style of window treatment, and whether the draperies (if used) are to draw or be stationary panels. If you are making draperies, you also need to decide whether to make the pleats by hand or to use one of the pleat tapes available. The commonest kind of pleat tape has pockets into which four-pronged hooks are inserted, which pull the fabric into folds. You can also buy tape containing cords, which pull it and the fabric into different kinds of pleats. However, if you are using heavy fabric or have a special effect in mind, you will need to make the pleats by hand. In some cases, calculating the positioning of pleats will be easier if you opt for a hand-pleated heading.

CALCULATING FABRIC QUANTITY

Each Fabric Length

Measure the finished length of the draperies and add the appropriate allowances for the hem and your choice of heading. For example, you will need 6 inches (15 cm) for a double bottom hem and 3 inches (7.5 cm) for a simple heading. The allowances are given where appropriate in the following pages. Allow extra material for patterned fabric by adding one repeat to each length.

Number of Fabric Widths

For draperies with heading tape:

1 Measure the length of the rod or pole and divide in half for two panels.

2 Add 4 inches (10 cm) for the side hems on one panel. Add another 4 inches (10 cm) for the overlap in the middle.

3 Multiply this width by the amount of fullness appropriate for the heading style. For example, simple shirring tape requires one-and-a-half times the rod length; cartridge pleat tapes two-and-a-quarter times the length; and pinch pleats two-and-a-half times the length. However, the fullness needed will be indicated by the manufacturer.

4 Divide this total width by the fabric width. Most fabrics are 47 inches (120 cm), 48 inches (122 cm), 54 inches (137 cm), 55 inches (140 cm) or 59 inches (150 cm) wide. Round off the resulting figure to the nearest whole number to work out the number of fabric widths each panel will take.

For draperies with hand-pleated headings:

1 Measure the length of the rod or pole. Divide in half for two panels. Add 4 inches (10 cm) for the side hems on each panel and another 4 inches (10 cm) for the overlap in the middle.

2 Work out the number of pleats and spaces that will fit the draperies with about 6 inches (15 cm) for each pleat and a space of 4¾ inches (12 cm) between each pleat. Divide the width of the panel

(minus the side hems and center overlap) by 4¾ inches (12 cm). Round off to the nearest number. So, if you have eight gaps, make nine pleats.

3 Work out the fabric for the pleats by multiplying the number of pleats by 6 inches (15 cm).

4 Add this figure to the total panel width (including the side hems and center overlap) and add an additional 4¾ inches (12 cm) for the return on the outer edge of each panel. (This will vary, depending on the position of the rod.) Round off to the nearest whole number.

5 Divide the resulting figure by the width of the fabric. Round off to the nearest whole number to find out the number of fabric widths for each panel.

Final Fabric Estimate

Multiply the overall panel length by the number of fabric widths for both panels to give the final fabric amount. Allow another 1 inch (2.5 cm) for every yard (meter) of non-preshrunk fabric.

CUTTING OUT THE FABRIC

Cut out all fabrics on a flat, clean surface. If you are using fabrics with a high sheen or a pile, mark the top of each length so that the texture will run in the same direction. Cut straight across the fabric at right angles to the selvage to ensure that the finished draperies hang straight. Make one end straight by pulling a thread across the weave and cutting along it, or use a right-angle triangle to mark a line on the fabric with a pencil and a rule.

Measure the length of the first width down each selvage and mark with pins. Fold the fabric along the pin line and cut along the fold. If the fabric has a large pattern, work out the length so that the hemline will come below a complete motif. It is much better to let a partial motif occur at the top of the draperies where it will not be so obvious. Cut the number of widths required for each panel in the same way. Make sure that on a patterned fabric each length starts at the same point and place half widths at the outer edges of the panels.

MAKING UNLINED DRAPERIES

Although most draperies hang better when they are lined, sometimes unlined draperies are more suitable. They are one of the easiest types of drapery to make and can produce sophisticated results. When estimating the fabric for unlined draperies, allow for a 6-inch (15-cm) hem and 2½ inches (6 cm) for each side hem. The heading allowance and total width will depend on the kind of heading tape you are using. The instructions that follow assume a 2¾-inch (7-cm) heading allowance.

1 Join widths and any half widths with a flat seam, matching the pattern if necessary. Trim off the selvages to prevent them from puckering the seam. Press each of the seams open.

2 Turn in and press double 1-inch (2.5-cm) hems along each side edge. Pin and baste these edges to within 2¾ inches (7 cm) of the top edge and 6 inches (15 cm) of the bottom edge.

3 Turn up and press 6 inches (15 cm) along the bottom edge. Press in a miter at each corner and then turn in and press the raw edge to make a double 3-inch (7.5-cm) hem. Machine-stitch the side hems, or sew by hand with a loose slipstitch. Stitch the mitered corners followed by the bottom hem, using the same loose slipstitch or catchstitch. Weight the draperies by sewing weighted tape into the hem or lead weights in the corners.

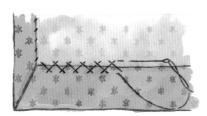

Adding Simple Shirring Tape

Loosely shirred headings can be used for very informal draperies made of lightweight fabric. You can buy strips of shirring tape, which measure 1 inch (2.5 cm) in depth and create a frill of fabric above the rod and loose gathers below. You can, of course, alter the depth of the upper frill by allowing for a deeper top hem.

1 To apply the tape, turn down and press along the top edge of the fabric by 2¾ inches (7 cm), mitering the corners. Cut the tape to the width of the panel with another 2 inches (5 cm) for side hems. Turn under 1 inch (2.5 cm) of the tape at each end and pin and baste the tape to the wrong side so that the tape covers the raw edge of the hem.

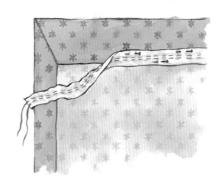

2 Machine-stitch the tape along its top and bottom edges, stitching in the same direction. Sew the ends of the shirring tape in place by hand. Use the drawstrings to gather up the drapery so that it fits the rod; arrange the gathers evenly across the width of the drapery. Knot the strings at one end of the tape to hold the gathers in place. Fit hooks into the row of woven loops on the tape and hang the draperies from the rod.

Adding Cartridge Pleat Tape

Cartridge pleat tape, which gathers the fabric into thin vertical folds, is available in 3-inch (7.5-cm) and 4–5-inch (10–13-cm) widths, and in different weights for heavy and lightweight fabrics. This tape has three rows of pockets for inserting the hooks.

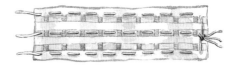

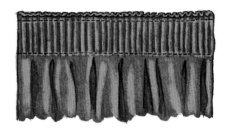

1 Cartridge pleat tapes are applied in much the same way as shirring tape, but the tape is positioned almost at the top of the drapery. If you wish, you can gather the tape first, before attaching it to the drapery, marking the position of the pleats on the tape with a pencil. Open out the tape and apply as usual. Do not put a pleat at the outer edges of the drapery, where a single hook will be.

2 Smooth out the tape and sew it to the drapery. Pull up the pleats again, according to your earlier pencil marks, secure the drawstrings, fit hooks into the loops, and hang the draperies from the rod.

MAKING LINED DRAPERIES

Lining draperies is important if you wish to protect the main fabric from sunlight and dampness and also to improve the hang of the drapery. Cotton sateen lining fabric is relatively inexpensive and is available in cream, beige, and white. In some places it is also possible to buy colored sateen to complement your drapery.

Standard Lining

This is the simplest method for lining draperies, but remember to add allowances on the drapery fabric for the side hems, the bottom hem, and your choice of heading tape. Cut out the lining to the size of the finished drapery and make sure that the drapery fabric is approximately 5 inches (13 cm) wider and 9 inches (23 cm) longer than the lining.

1 Join the widths and any half widths of drapery fabric and lining fabric as for standard unlined draperies. Place the lining on top of the drapery panel with right sides facing so that the top of the lining is 3 inches (7.5 cm) below the top of the drapery fabric. Pin the side edges of the drapery and the lining together as shown below and then machine-stitch ½ inch (1 cm) in from the edge. The stitching should run from 3 inches (7.5 cm) below the top of the lining to within 6 inches (15 cm) of the bottom edge. Remove the selvages or notch the seam allowances in order to reduce bulk.

2 Turn up and press 2 inches (5 cm) to the wrong side along the bottom edge of the lining. Make a double 1-inch (2.5-cm) hem and machine-stitch. Turn up and press 6 inches (15 cm) to the wrong side of the main fabric, press in the mitered corners, and baste a double 3-inch (7.5-cm) hem.

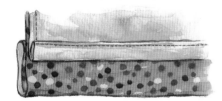

3 Turn the fabric and lining right side out, centering the lining to create an equal border of fabric along each side of the lining. Slipstitch the remaining side edges of the lining to the drapery, leaving some of the lining free at the top so that you can turn in the mitered corners of the main fabric.

Stitch the lower miters and hem of the drapery and remove the basting, as for an unlined drapery.

4 Turn down and press 3 inches (7.5 cm) along the top of the drapery, covering the lining, and press in and slipstitch the miters. Pin and baste the heading tape of your choice in place across the top of the drapery, following the instructions on page 164. Machine-stitch the heading tape in place.

Locked-In Lining

This particular lining method is preferred by professional drapery makers because it ensures that the draperies hang beautifully. When measuring for unfinished panels, make sure to allow an extra 5 inches (13 cm) in width and 9 inches (23 cm) in length than the finished flat drapery panel. The lining should be approximately 1¾ inches (4 cm) smaller all the way around than the drapery.

1 Join the drapery and lining widths as for draperies with an ordinary lining. Turn in and press 2½ inches (6 cm) down each side edge of the drapery and 6 inches (15 cm) along the bottom edge. Press in the miters at the bottom corners of the drapery. Loosely slipstitch the side hems, and sew the miters in place. Slipstitch or catchstitch the hem as for unlined draperies. Lay the fabric right side down. Draw a series of parallel vertical lines about every 12 inches (30 cm) using some tailor's chalk, or a pencil, and a yardstick.

Place the lining right side up on top of the drapery fabric so that its top edge is ¾ inch (2 cm) below the top edge of the drapery panel. Fold back one side edge of the lining lengthwise to the first chalk mark. Slipstitch or lock-stitch the lining to the

drapery, starting 7 inches (18 cm) down from the top of the drapery and joining them with large, loose stitches. Continue down the lining to the top of the drapery's bottom hem.

2 Smooth the lining out again. Fold back the other side edge of the lining to the next chalk line. Slipstitch or lock-stitch this line to the drapery. Repeat for each line across the drapery.

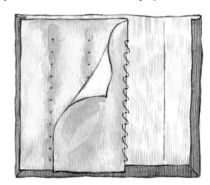

3 Turn in and press ¾ inch (2 cm) along the side edges of the lining and 1¾ inches (4 cm) along the bottom edge. Slipstitch the lining in place on the drapery along these three edges. Turn under and press 3 inches (7.5 cm) along the drapery's top edge and 2¾ inches (7 cm) along the top edge of the lining. Miter all corners, slipstitch in place, and then apply the heading tape of your choice.

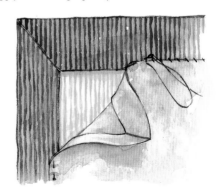

HAND-SEWN HEADINGS

Ready-made heading tapes achieve elegant results, but headings that are made by hand are neater, more precise, and more professional looking. There are a number of different styles to choose from, including pinch pleats, French pleats, and cartridge pleats, some of which are described here.

Pinch Pleats

These are by far the most popular kind of drapery pleat. You can buy tape to form these pleats, but making them by hand produces a crisper effect. The following instructions include an interlining. Though seldom seen in the United States, it produces a rich effect—and conserves heat. Table felt or flannelette can be used for this purpose.

1 To pleat the draperies by hand, measure the fabric quantities very carefully. You will need drapery fabric with a 4-inch (10-cm) bottom hem allowance and a 4-inch (10-cm) top hem allowance. Remember to include extra if you need to match the design on different widths of patterned fabric. When working out the number of fabric widths to buy, you will need to calculate the number of pleats and spaces that will fit each panel and also take the side returns, any center overlap, and the side hems into account (see "Calculating Fabric Quantity," page 163).

You will also need to make a lining panel measuring the width of the unpleated drapery with no side allowances, a ¾-inch (2-cm) top hem and a 1¾-inch (4-cm) hem allowance; a piece of interlining cut to the same size as the finished drapery panel, and a strip of interfacing cut to the same width as the finished drapery and at least 4 inches (10 cm) wide to ensure that the pleats maintain their shape.

2 Turn under 4 inches (10 cm) along the top edge of the drapery panel and position the top edge of the interfacing so that it lines up with the fold line. Catchstitch the interfacing to the drapery. Lay the piece of interlining over the interfacing, and lock-stitch in place. Turn the top edge and the

2-inch (5-cm) side hems of the drapery panel over the interlining, mitering the corners, and catchstitch. Turn up and stitch a ¾-inch (2-cm) double hem along the bottom of the lining and turn under and press ¾ inch (2 cm) along the top and side edges. Lock-stitch the lining to the interlining and slipstitch the folded top and side edges of the lining to the drapery panel.

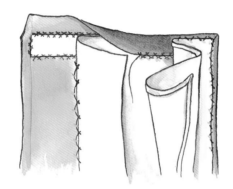

3 Turn up the 4-inch (10-cm) bottom drapery hem, mitering the corners as usual, and slipstitch the hem in place beneath the lining.

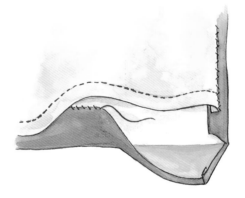

4 Using a pencil or tailor's chalk, mark the position of the returns, the pleats, the spaces, and the center overlap on the back of the panel according to your earlier calculations.

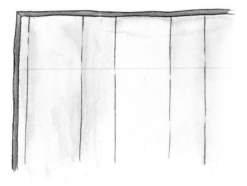

5 Fold and stitch the pleat lines to the depth of the interfacing. Form the pleats by hand and stitch to ½ inch (1 cm) below the interfacing. Stitch across the pleats at the top or hold in place with pin hooks.

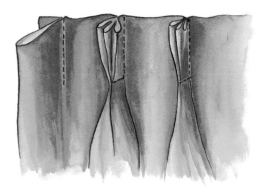

6 Fix hooks to the pleats and side edges. Hang from rings as shown or from traverse rod sliders.

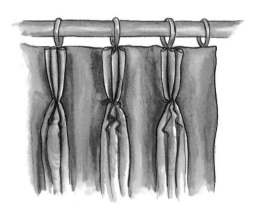

French, or Goblet, Pleats

Often used for stationary panels, French, or goblet, pleats can be decorated with cords, buttons, or tassels. Follow the instructions for pinch pleats, but once you have folded and stitched along the pleat lines, open out the pleats and hand-stitch around the base. Roll up strips of interfacing and wedge into each pleat to give it shape.

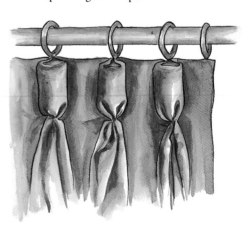

Cartridge Pleats

This simple-looking heading requires less fabric for each pleat but is made in the same way as pinch or French pleats. Follow the instructions for pinch pleats, again working out the number of pleats and spaces for each panel carefully, but after stitching the pleats, open them out fully and insert equal-size pieces of rolled-up interfacing into each to produce the neatly rounded shape.

Rod Casing

This type of heading is used for curtains such as tieback or fiberglass curtains. The casing simply runs across the top of the curtain and slips over a simple or adjustable curtain rod.

1   Measure the curtain material as for unlined draperies (page 164) and allow for a top hem of 4 inches (10 cm) and a bottom hem of 6 inches (15 cm). Unless you are using very sheer fabric, the width of the curtains should be about two times the length of the rod. If you are using extra-sheer fabric, allow more.

Join the widths of curtain fabric as for unlined draperies, making the side hems and double bottom hem as usual. Turn under and press 4 inches (10 cm) along the top of the curtain and make a double hem measuring 2 inches (5 cm) on the bottom. Machine-stitch along the bottom edge and then stitch a second line 1 inch (2.5 cm) above the first line. If you are using a thick rod, you will need to allow extra fabric to make a casing that is wide enough to take the rod and to ensure that the ruffle is in proportion to the rest of the curtain. As a rule, this measures about 1 inch (2.5 cm), so you should allow 2 inches (5 cm) for the double thickness.

2   Slip the rod or wire through the casing and hang the curtain.

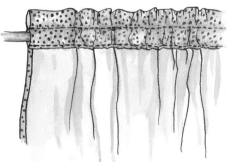

Scalloped Heading

This heading is fairly plain. The instructions are for a flat curtain; allow for fullness, if required.

1   Measure and make up the curtain as for unlined draperies (page 164) but leave the top and bottom edges unfinished. Allow only ¼ inch (5 mm) at the top of the panel for the hem. Work out how many scallops will fit across the panel, with each scallop measuring about 3 inches (7.5 cm). Allow for ¾ inch (2 cm) between each scallop and an equal amount of fabric on either side of the panel.

2   Make a scallop template by drawing a circle with a 1¾-inch (4-cm) radius on cardboard. Draw a

rectangle using the diameter of the circle as a base. The sides of the rectangle should measure 2½ inches (6 cm). Cut out the whole template.

3   Draw around the template along the width of the panel, on the wrong side of the fabric, with a pencil, leaving 1 inch (2.5 cm) between each scallop and equal spaces at either end.

4   Make a facing by cutting out a 6-inch- (15-cm-) wide strip of fabric, ½ inch (1 cm) longer than the width of the finished panel. Turn in each short end of the facing by approximately ¼ inch (5 mm). Press flat and baste along these ends. With right sides together, baste the facing to the top of the curtain. Turn up the bottom edge of the facing by ¼ inch (5 mm) and press and baste. With the wrong side of the curtain fabric facing you, baste through the panel and facing along the outline of the scallops, with a straight line of basting between them, about ¼ inch (5 mm) in from the edge. Machine-stitch along this basting line. Cut out the scallops, making sure to stop ¼ inch (5 mm) short of the stitching, and cut notches in the material to reduce bulk (see "Curved Seams," page 180).

5   Turn the curtain and facing right side out and press flat. Slipstitch the side and bottom edges of the facing in place. The curtain can be hung in a number of informal ways. You can simply sew metal curtain rings to the center of the spaces between each scallop as shown below. Alternatively, you can buy decorative metal clips that you fix onto both the curtain and the metal curtain rings. Slip the pole through these curtain rings. Hold the finished curtain up against the window in order to check the length of the hem, then pin, baste, and slipstitch the hem in place. Press the finished curtain, then slip the rings over your choice of pole. Hang the curtain.

OTHER DRAPERY STYLES

The following ideas show the wide variety of curtains and draperies that can be made.

Tab Headings

This is a simple heading style for a pair of curtains and is also suitable for wall hangings.

1 Make the curtains as usual, but leave the top and bottom edges unfinished, allowing only ½ inch (1 cm) at the top for a hem.

2 First find the length of the tab by measuring the circumference of the rod, adding another 3 inches (7.5 cm) for seam allowances. Each finished tab should measure about 2–3 inches (5–7.5 cm) in width with 1 inch (2.5 cm) for seams. Decide on the number of tabs you will need, as for scalloped headings. Make enough tabs so they can be spaced every 4 inches (10 cm) along the width of the curtain, starting 1 inch (2.5 cm) in from either end.

3 Cut strips for the tabs to the required length and width. Keeping right sides together, fold each strip in half lengthwise and make a ½-inch (1-cm) seam down the long edge, leaving the ends open. Turn right side out and refold so that the seam is at the back of the strip in the center. Press flat.

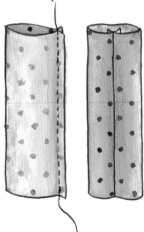

4 Fold the tabs in half widthwise and pin at the correct spacing to the right side of the curtain, matching the raw edges. Baste in place ½ inch (1 cm) from the edge.

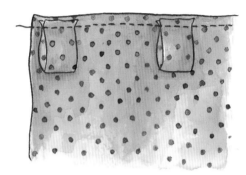

5 Cut a 3-inch (7.5-cm) strip of fabric ½ inch (1 cm) wider than the curtain to make a facing. Turn in ¼ inch (5 mm) on each short end, press, and baste. With right sides facing, baste the facing to the top of the curtain. Turn up ¼ inch (5 mm) along the bottom edge of the facing; press and baste. Baste and stitch along the top of the curtain ½ inch (1 cm) from the edge through all the fabric including tabs. Turn right side out and press flat.

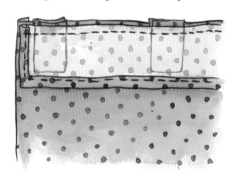

6 Slipstitch the side and bottom edges of the facing to the main fabric and slip the rod through the tabs. Temporarily hang the curtain to check the hem length. Pin and baste the bottom hem and slipstitch in place. Press flat before hanging.

Tab Heading with Buttons

You can create a variety of decorative effects with tabs. For example, the tabs can be made from material contrasting with the curtain or tabs in different colors can be alternated across the width of the curtain. You might also like to embellish the tabs with buttons, brocade, ribbons, or bows. These decorative effects are all easily achieved, particularly if you enjoy experimenting with different trimmings and finishes. The striking method shown below is ideal for full-length but informal draperies.

1 Make a curtain or drapery panel as usual and sew the tabs to the back at regular intervals.

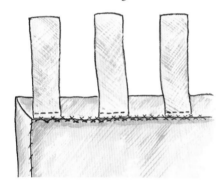

2 Fold the tabs to the front and sew a button to the center of each tab through all thicknesses.

3 Hang the curtain from a decorative pole.

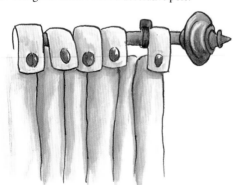

A Valance-Trimmed Drapery

Follow the instructions on pages 163 for measuring and cutting out the draperies. For the valance, cut out an extra length of both the drapery fabric and the lining to the same width as the drapery. The depth of the valance will depend on the length of the drapery, but allow approximately 10 inches (25 cm) for a 6-foot (2-m) drapery.

1 Make the draperies, leaving the top edges of the drapery fabric and the lining unfinished. With right sides together, sew the side seams of the valance and its lining. Turn right side out; press.

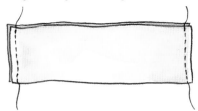

2 Placing the right side of the valance to the wrong side of the drapery, pin, baste, and stitch across the top of the drapery and valance, leaving a ½-inch (1-cm) seam allowance. Fold in each end of this seam and hand-sew to finish.

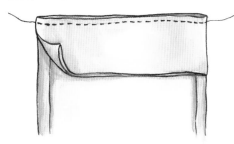

3 Turn the valance over to the right side of the drapery and press the seam. Finish the bottom of the valance by tucking the raw edges to the inside and sewing a length of fringe across it as shown.

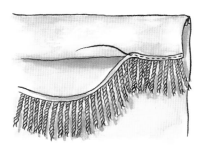

4 Sew approximately twelve rings to the top of the curtain and thread onto a wooden or cast-iron pole.

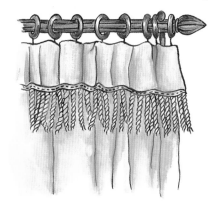

Other Valance Trimmings

You may like to sew a strip of bobbles across the bottom edge of the valance, or make both the drapery and the valance from sheer fabric (see below).

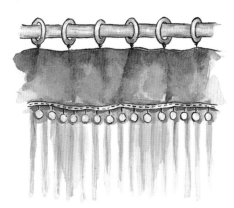

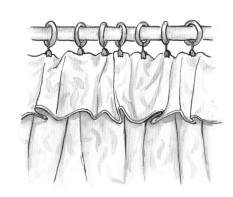

A Fixed Hook Portière

Follow the instructions on page 163 for measuring and cutting out draperies, leaving a ½ inch (1-cm) seam allowance. Allow approximately two times the width of the doorway for the drapery width. Line the portière with the same fabric or contrasting fabric to make it attractive from both sides.

1 With right sides facing, pin, baste, and stitch the two pieces of fabric together around the bottom and side edges with a ½-inch (1-cm) seam. Turn right side out and press flat. Make the loops by folding fabric strips in half lengthwise. Baste and machine-stitch in place between the fabric pieces.

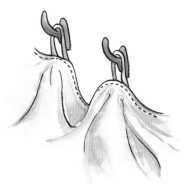

2 Hang the loops over hooks fixed to the door frame; hold the portière in place with a tieback.

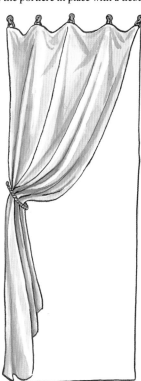

Eyelet Headings

Eyelet headings are perfect for decorative curtains or draperies that are not pulled back very often. They are one of those simple but effective finishing touches that can turn the most ordinary window treatment into something special.

The eyelets can be threaded over a wooden or brass pole for an understated effect; or you can use string or ribbons threaded through the eyelets to suspend the curtains or draperies.

The headings should always be stiffened with a strip of interfacing for added crispness. The stiffening fabric is hand- or machine-stitched between the fabric and the lining or inserted into a folded heading. If your draperies are unlined, they will need a facing in order to hide the stiffening. You can buy the grommets used to finish the eyelets in a variety of sizes from most department stores or notions stores. They are accompanied by a small gun for punching the grommets through the fabric.

Simple Eyelets

Having stiffened the top of the drapery with a strip of interfacing when making the draperies, punch ¾-inch (20-mm) grommets through the fabric according to the manufacturer's instructions and thread onto a suitable pole.

Eyelets with Cords or Ribbons

When measuring for the drapery fabric, add 4 inches (10 cm) to the total drapery length. Turn under 2½ inches (6 cm) on the top edge of the drapery. Open out and place a 2-inch (5-cm) strip of interfacing against the fold line. Cover over the interfacing with the drapery fabric and slipstitch

into place. Once you have completed the draperies, punch ⅜-inch (10-mm) grommets into the fabric and thread double cords through them as shown.

Alternatively, insert ¾-inch (20-mm) grommets and tie the drapery to the pole using 12-inch (30-cm) ribbons tied into bows as shown below.

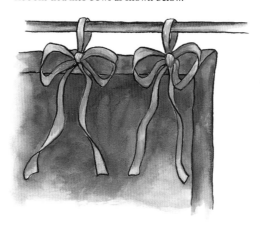

Shower Curtains

These are easy to make from waterproof fabrics; or use normal fabric with a plastic inner curtain. Most shower curtains should be made to a fullness of one-and-a-half times the length of the shower rod. A hemmed shower curtain can also have metal rings sewn along the top every 4 inches (10 cm), which can then be slid over a shower rod.

1 When cutting out the fabric and inner curtain, allow for 1-inch (2.5-cm) double side hems and a 2-inch (5-cm) double hem along the bottom. Add a ½ inch (1-cm) seam allowance across the top edge.

2 Turn under 1-inch (2.5-cm) double hems down the sides and a 2-inch (5-cm) double hem across the bottom edge of the fabric and inner curtain, mitering the corners, and stitch. Place the lining on

top of the fabric with right sides together and stitch a seam ½ inch (1 cm) below the top raw edges. Turn the fabric right side out and press the seams flat.

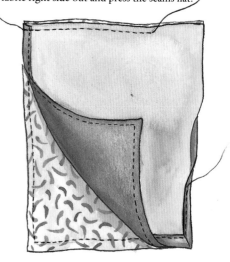

3 If the shower rod is not stationary, stitch a casing to accommodate it, positioning the upper row of stitching ½ inch (1 cm) from the top edge.

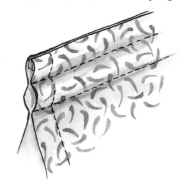

4 For an unlined shower curtain, turn under the top edge by 1 inch (2.5 cm) and insert grommets every 6 inches (15 cm) as shown below.

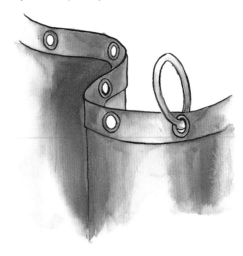

SWAGS AND CASCADES

Swags and cascades can be fixed to a shelf above the window although many are threaded on a second pole that extends beyond the curtain rod, or on the curtain rod itself. The method shown here uses a shelf fixed above the window as for valances (page 172). When making swags and cascades, use an old sheet to make a pattern. This will give a visual and mathematical idea of the degree of drape.

1 The upper edge of the swag piece should be about 10 inches (25 cm) shorter than the shelf, while the bottom edge should be about 8 inches (20 cm) longer, although this depends on the depth of swag you want. Pin the swag piece across the top of the shelf and gather the ends until you are happy with the effect. Mark the material with tailor's chalk where it folds over the front of the shelf, as well as the depth of the ungathered swag.

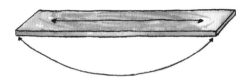

2 Open out the swag piece and mark the seam-lines, using the chalk marks as guides. Use this as a pattern to cut out the fabric, allowing for a 1-inch (2.5-cm) hem along the top and bottom edges and 1 inch (2.5 cm) for gathering and finishing down the angled sides. Make the swag and the lining as for normal lined draperies, treating the top and bottom edges of the swag as if they were the sides of a drapery panel.

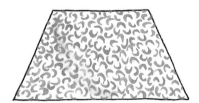

3 To make the pattern for the cascades, work out the width and spacing for the fold lines with a tape measure held against the shelf. Decide on the inner and outer lengths of the folds in the cascades. Transfer these measurements to the fabric pattern. Cut out the cascade pattern and check for fit.

4 Use the fabric cascade pattern in order to cut out the cascades from drapery fabric, allowing ¾ inch (2 cm) for seams around the sides and bottom edge and 4 inches (10 cm) along the top edge. Place the lining on top of the main cascade piece with right sides facing. Stitch all around the sides and bottom edges. Trim the seams, press, and turn right side out.

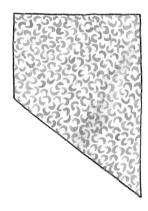

5 Run two rows of gathering stitches along the angled sides of the swag panel and pin to the shelf to check the effect. Staple to the top of the shelf.

6 Mark and press the pleats in place on the two cascade panels, using the fabric cascade patterns as a guide. Stitch the pleats by hand and staple the cascades to the top of the shelf as shown.

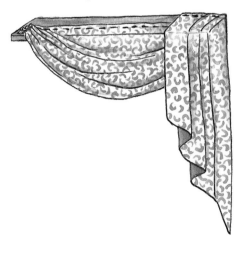

7 The swag and cascades can be used alone at a window or in conjunction with a pair of draperies. You can, of course, use different fabrics for the swag and the cascades to create dramatic effects.

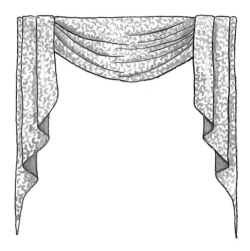

Swag Alternatives

There are a number of attractive ways of varying the classic swag and cascades just described. For example, a swag does not necessarily have to be accompanied by a pair of cascades. You may simply prefer to make the swag and cascades from one large piece of fabric, as shown below, draping the fabric over a pole and stapling it in place. The look can be harmonized still further by adding a decorative trimming, such as fringe, bobbles, or braid, along the edge of the swag and down the inside of the cascades. Alternatively, you could stitch the swag to a pair of straight draperies made with a rod casing.

VALANCES

Valances can be fixed to a shelf above the window frame and made in a variety of styles—straight, shaped, gathered, or pleated. You can design the shape of the valance after the shelf is up, making sure that the shelf is wide enough to cover the width of the window frame. A general rule of proportion is that the valance should be up to one-sixth of the height of the window, but for a more dramatic effect, you can make it a little deeper.

Cutting Out the Fabric

For a shaped valance, cut out the main fabric so that it is approximately 2 inches (5 cm) larger than the template all the way around (see "Making a Template"). Cut out a piece of lining, interlining (optional), and interfacing, all the same size as the template.

Fixing the Shelf

First decide on the position of the shelf. You can either fit it close to the frame around the window or make it wider and fit it above the window, in order to make the window seem larger. The draperies themselves will hang inside the box, so make sure that there is enough room for the draperies to stack back when opened.

Fit the shelf with angle irons, or screw it directly to the wooden window frame if possible. Use ½-inch (1-cm) plywood or softwood that is at least 4 inches (10 cm) wide. Cut the wood to the same length as the curtain rod, adding another 2 inches (5 cm) for clearance. To create the box, screw 4-inch- (10-cm-) square pieces of wood to each end of the shelf before fixing the shelf in place.

Making a Template

Make a pattern for the valance by trimming a sheet of paper a little larger than the finished length of the valance including the two side pieces. Fold in half down the center. Draw the shape along the bottom of the folded paper and cut out. Unfold the paper and try it against the board for size and effect.

If you are making a gathered or pleated valance with heading tape, remember you will have to elongate any shaping you design to allow for the fullness of the fabric. To do this, cut a second paper template to the finished size of the valance before gathering. Take measurements down the length of the first template, every 4 inches (10 cm) or so, and transfer these to the second one. Spread these measurements apart on the second template as appropriate for the heading tape. Some pinch pleat tapes, for instance, need two-and-a-quarter times the finished width, so allow for this when transferring the shape to the second template.

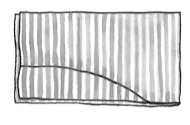

Making a Shaped Valance

1 Lock-stitch the piece of interlining (optional) to the wrong side of the main fabric. Center the interfacing over the interlining and catchstitch in place all around the edge.

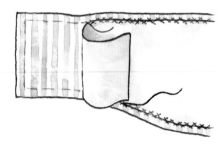

2 Fold the seam allowance of the main fabric over the interfacing, mitering the corners. Clip the seam allowance and catchstitch in place.

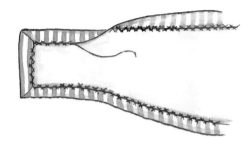

3 Turn under the seam allowance all around the lining so that it is about ½ inch (1 cm) smaller than the main panel of the valance. Slipstitch the folded hem of the lining to the seam allowance all the way around the main panel. Glue one strip of hook-and-loop tape to the edge of the shelf and stitch the other strip to the back of the valance for sticking directly to the board. Fix the valance to the shelf.

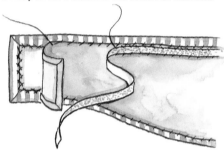

4 There are a variety of ways in which you can fix the valance to the board. For example, you can use ½-inch (1-cm) tacks, which are then concealed with a strip of fabric or braid. The fabric is simply glued over the tacks with a special fabric glue. You can also use screw eyes, which are fitted around the outer edge of the underside of the shelf, from which you hang hooks fixed to the inside of the valance.

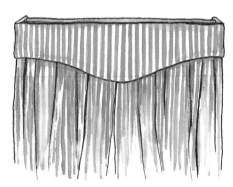

Decorative Alternatives

Valances are the ideal way to add a personal touch to a window treatment. Shaped valances enable you to devise your own imaginative designs, which are easy to apply to a template. Choose from among the ideas shown below, which range from curved valances to those with zigzag points. Valances can also be pleated or gathered to create a decorative effect across the top of a plain pair of draperies. Both shaped and pleated or gathered valances can be edged with trimmings.

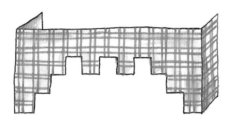

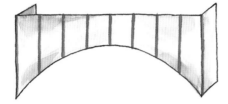

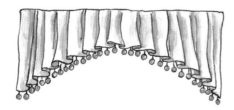

A Gathered Valance

For a gathered valance you will need a piece of fabric measuring twice the finished width of the valance plus a piece of fabric cut the same size as the finished width for the top border. You will also need a similar amount of lining, a piece of contrasting fabric to edge the bottom of the valance, and some interfacing to stiffen the top border.

1 Make the top border as you would a shaped valance (page 172) but leave the lower edge straight and unfinished.

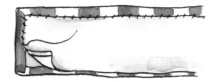

2 Add a band of contrasting fabric, which should measure approximately 3 inches (7.5 cm) in depth, to form a border along the bottom of the gathered part of the valance.

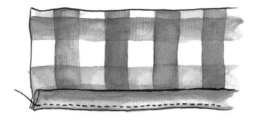

3 Sew a lining to the side edges of the gathered part of the valance as you would a conventional drapery with a standard lining (page 164) but leave the top edge and stitch the hem.

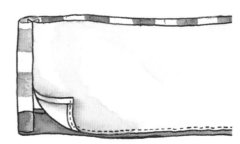

4 Sew two rows of gathering stitches about ½ inch (1 cm) down from the top edge of the gathered part of the valance. Draw the stitches up in order to create the gathers until the valance is the right width for the top border.

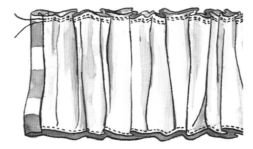

5 Pin, then machine-stitch together the top border and the gathered edge of the valance with right sides together. Stitch through both the main fabric and the lining of the gathered section but only through the main fabric of the top border.

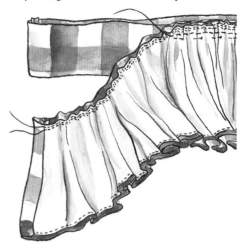

6 Tuck the seam allowances into the lining of the top border and hand-stitch to finish.

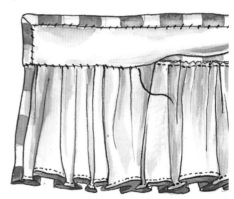

7 Press the valance, paying special attention to the gathered part. If you are using hook-and-loop tape, sew it 1 inch (2.5 cm) from the top of the valance. Attach the valance to the shelf.

SHADES

Practical and decorative, window shades keep out the light and protect delicate fabrics.

Roller Shades

These are the simplest shades to make and consist of fabric wound around a wooden roller attached at the top of the window. The shade can be pulled down to produce a flat screen over the window. When released it winds around the roller unless locked into position. Roller shades are ideal for sloping windows and can be secured at the bottom with a hook. Roller-shade kits typically contain a wooden roller with a square pin at one end and a round pin attached to a pin cap; two brackets for fixing the roller in place, either to the side or the front of the window frame; a wooden batten for slipping through the casing; a cord holder and cord for adjusting the level of the shade.

To work out the amount of fabric, measure the length of the window and add 8 inches (20 cm) for the batten casing as well as enough fabric to cover the roller when the shade is down. To find the width of the roller and fabric that you need, measure the width of the window and add 2 inches (5 cm) to each side. If you want the shade to hang inside the recess, measure the width of the window and subtract the space needed for the brackets. You probably will not be able to buy a kit to fit the exact dimensions of the shade so buy the next size up.

Cutting Out the Fabric

There are special fabrics available for shades that do not fray and are stiff and fade resistant, although ordinary fabrics can be stiffened with a liquid or aerosol stiffening agent. If you decide on this method, test a piece of sample fabric to see how it responds and stiffen the fabric before cutting out in case of shrinkage. Cut out the fabric for the shade to the measurements of the roller, making sure that you cut the fabric out straight (a right-angle triangle is useful here), so that the shade will hang correctly and roll up freely. If you dislike the raw edges, turn in a narrow hem on each side edge before stiffening the fabric and bond with fusible web.

Assembling the Roller Shade

1 Fix the metal brackets to the wall or window frame, depending on how you have decided to hang the shade. Often, the square, slotted bracket is positioned on the left and the round-hole bracket on the right so that the rolled-up fabric is visible at the top, but check the manufacturer's instructions first.

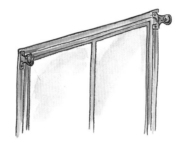

2 Measure the distance between the brackets to find the length of the roller and the wooden batten, then cut them down to size. Position the metal end plate, which comes with the roller-shade kit, over the cut end of the roller and tap in the pin.

3 Cut out the fabric, then turn over and stitch a casing across the bottom of the shade, deep enough to take the wooden batten. Insert the batten into the casing.

4 Attach the cord and cord holder with screws to the wooden batten as shown below.

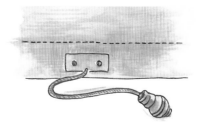

5 Turn over a narrow allowance at the top of the shade. With the right side of the fabric facing you and the round pin on the right, roll the turned edge over the roller and fix in place with ¼ inch (5-mm) tacks spaced approximately every 2 inches (5 cm). Roll up the shade and then hang it by attaching it to the brackets. To test the shade, pull it down and then remove it from the brackets. Roll it up halfway, hang, and pull it down again. Keep taking the shade down and rolling it up until it will roll easily to the top of the window when released.

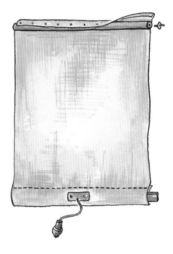

Decorative Edgings

Roller shades can be decorated with a variety of trimmings such as ribbons, fringe, or braid. Stiffened fabric is difficult to pin, so simply tape the ribbon or fringe to the wrong side of the shade, stitch through the tape and fabric, and then remove the tape. An equally attractive, but slightly more complicated, alternative is to shape the edge of the shade, as described below.

1 Sew a tuck about 3–6 inches (7.5–15 cm) from the edge of the shade for the wooden batten, thus leaving a strip of fabric below the batten.

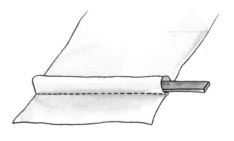

2 Take a piece of paper the same size as this edge. Fold in half, draw the design, and cut out.

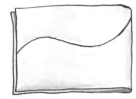

3 Open out the pattern and tape it to the wrong side of the edge. Pencil around the shape, cut out neatly, and finish with zigzag stitch.

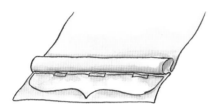

4 You can make other edgings using different template designs. Fold the paper accordion style, draw the design on the top, cut out, and trace.

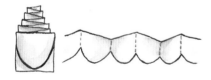

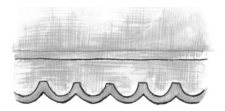

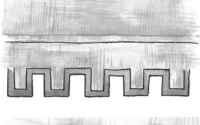

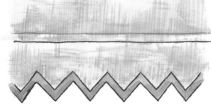

Roman Shades

Roman shades, which come in a number of styles, are operated by a system of vertical cords slotted through ringed tapes at the back of the shade. Roman shades can either hang outside the window frame, so that the entire frame is covered, or fit into the recess of the window. In the latter case, they can perhaps be combined with curtains.

To make a standard Roman shade, you will need two pieces of fabric measuring the width and length of the window, but add another 3½ inches (9 cm) to the length and 4½ inches (11.5 cm) to the width if the shade is to hang outside the window frame (if it is to hang inside the frame, add only 1 inch [2.5 cm]); shade tapes (there are a variety of tapes available with loops or rings fixed at regular intervals); nylon shade cord to thread through each vertical row of loops (each length should be twice the shade length plus one width); screw eyes (you will need as many as there are rows of tape); a wooden batten, measuring ¾ x 2 inches (2 x 5 cm) thick; a lath, measuring 1¼ inches (3 cm) wide; hook-and-loop tape; angle irons for fixing the batten to the wall or window frame; and a wall cleat.

1 The Roman shade is fitted to the batten, so cut the batten to fit the width of the window and hang it from angle irons fixed to either side of the window frame. Using a staple gun or tacks, secure the toothed side of a strip of hook-and-loop tape to the top of the batten.

2 Take the two pieces of fabric, and, with right sides facing, pin, baste, and machine-stitch them together along the two long edges and one of the short edges, leaving a seam of ½ inch (1 cm). Turn right side out and press flat. Cut two pieces of ringed or looped shade tape the same length as the shade. The first ring or loop should be placed 6 inches (15 cm) from the top of the shade. Pin these pieces of tape along each side of the shade near the edge. Machine-stitch in place. Space the remaining tapes at intervals of approximately 12 inches (30 cm) between the first two tapes. Check that the loops on all the tapes are level across the width of the shade. Cut the tapes to length, pin, and machine-stitch.

3 Turn under ½ inch (1 cm) along the bottom edge and then another 1½ inches (4 cm) to enclose the ends of the tapes. Press and machine-stitch, taking care not to catch the rings or loops while stitching. Machine-stitch the hem close to this folded edge. Insert the lath into the casing and secure the ends with hand stitching. Turn under ½ inch (1 cm) along the top of the shade. Pin, baste, and machine-stitch the other portion of the hook-and-loop tape to conceal the raw edge of the fabric.

4 Cut the nylon cords to length for each tape. Tie one length of cord to the bottom ring of each row of tape and thread the cord up through every ring to the top ring. Fix a screw eye to the bottom edge of the batten above each row of tape. Attach the shade to the top of the batten with the hook-and-loop tape and run the cords through the screw eyes to meet on the far left. Trim the cords to length and knot together. Fix the batten above the window with angle irons. Screw the cleat to the window frame so that the cords can be secured.

BED FURNISHINGS

If you have a four-poster bed, the draperies can hang down each post or close around the bed. You can also include a valance around the top of the bed. If you want to create the effect of a four-poster with an ordinary bed, you will have to improvise by hanging poles from the ceiling joists or by fixing a curtain rod directly to the ceiling.

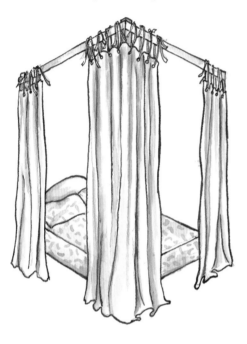

Dressing a Four-Poster Bed

1 First work out the amount of fabric for each drapery panel. To do this, measure the drop from the top of the post to floor level to determine the length and the distance around one corner of the bed to find the width. The distance will depend on how far you would like the draperies to draw around the bed. Use about one-and-a-half times the fabric fullness. Add a 4-inch (10-cm) top hem to the main length. You will also need a 2-inch (5-cm) strip of interfacing.

2 Make each drapery panel as for unlined draperies (page 164) but turn over the top edge by 2½ inches (6 cm). Open out and place the 2-inch (5-cm) strip of interfacing against the fold line. Cover the interfacing with the main fabric and slip-stitch in place. Punch ¾-inch (20-mm) grommets through the fabric and interfacing. Thread ties or ribbons through each eyelet and tie over the poles.

Corona Draperies

There are a variety of corona draperies to choose from which are fixed at the head of the bed. Corona draperies may be draped over a pole fixed either to the ceiling or to the wall; or they may be gathered and fixed to a coronet or semicircular bracket.

Simple Corona Draperies

1 The canopy is draped over a pole (fixed to a pole holder screwed to the ceiling joist or to a bracket in the wall) at right angles to the bed. The pole should be about 2 feet (60 cm) long, for which one width of fabric measuring 48 inches (122 cm) should be enough. If you would like more fullness, use more fabric widths and an equal amount of lining.

2 Measure from the top of the pole to the floor. Add at least 12 inches (30 cm) for looping the draperies into the tiebacks, plus 1 inch (2.5 cm) for the hem and ½ inch (1 cm) for the top seam. Double this measurement; multiply by the number of widths to find out how much fabric you need.

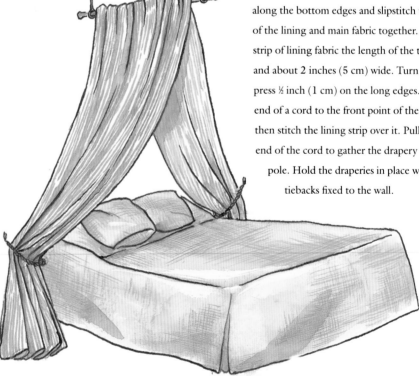

3 Cut the fabric into two equal lengths. If you would like extra fullness, cut two widths for each side and join the widths lengthwise, right sides facing, with a ½-inch (1-cm) seam; match the pattern if necessary. Remove the selvages, or cut notches in it, and press the seams flat. Lay the two pieces of material flat with right sides together and join across the top with a ½-inch (1-cm) seam. Make a panel of lining in the same way.

4 With right sides facing, stitch the lining to the main fabric along the sides edges, taking a ½-inch (1-cm) seam allowance. Turn right side out and press flat. Turn 1 inch (2.5 cm) to the inside along the bottom edges and slipstitch the edges of the lining and main fabric together. Cut a strip of lining fabric the length of the top seam and about 2 inches (5 cm) wide. Turn under and press ½ inch (1 cm) on the long edges. Sew one end of a cord to the front point of the seam, then stitch the lining strip over it. Pull the free end of the cord to gather the drapery over the pole. Hold the draperies in place with tiebacks fixed to the wall.

Coronet-Fixed Corona Draperies

These draperies, which are made up of a back drapery and two side draperies, hang from a coronet or semicircular bracket fixed to the wall usually 4–5 feet (1.2–1.4 m) above the bed. For a twin bed you will need two fabric widths for the back drapery; and for a double bed, three widths. Allow one or one-and-a-half widths for each side drapery, depending on how full you wish them to be.

1 Fix the coronet bracket to the wall with an angle iron. The bracket used here is made of 1-inch (2.5-cm) particleboard, measuring 16 inches (40 cm) across and about 10 inches (25 cm) deep. It has a curtain rod fixed to it so that the bed draperies can be made like ordinary draperies.

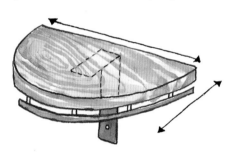

2 Measure the length of the draperies from the rod to the floor as for simple corona draperies. The draperies can either fall level with the floor or fall in staggered folds, as shown in the illustrations above. If you would like the draperies to fall in staggered folds, measure the edge of the side draperies against the wall as for corona draperies. If, on the other hand, you would like them to fall level with the floor, measure along the front edge of the side draperies instead. Add a 2-inch (5-cm) hem allowance and 1-inch (2.5-cm) top seam allowance to this initial length.

Draperies that fall in staggered folds

Draperies that are level with the floor

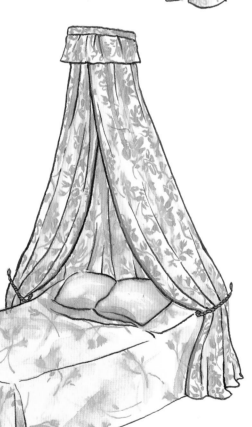

3 Make the back and side draperies as one large drapery, using the main fabric for both sides of the side draperies so that they look attractive from inside the bed. Use both the main fabric and the lining for the back drapery, with the lining facing the wall. Leave the hem unfinished if it is to hang level with the floor. Use shirring tape to gather the top edge. Gather the draperies to fit the coronet and hang the draperies from the rod. Screw ring holders to the wall for the tiebacks.

4 Mark the position of the tiebacks on the seamline between each side drapery and the back drapery. Unpick the seam here for about 6 inches (15 cm). Slipstitch the two layers of fabric around the slot.

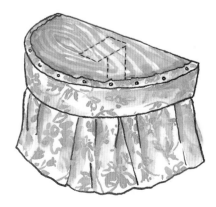

5 Hang the draperies and attach the tiebacks. If the draperies are to hang level with the floor, mark the hemline with pins. Remove the draperies from the rod and cut 2 inches (5 cm) below this line. Turn up a double 1-inch (2.5-cm) hem.

6 Make a valance for the corona bracket, which consists of a flat panel about 3½ inches (9 cm) deep and a 4½-inch (11-cm) ruffle. Tack or staple the valance to the top of the bracket as shown.

A Half Canopy

1 The total length of fabric should measure from the floor to the height at which the canopy will be attached to the wall (this will depend on the height of the ceiling but will be approximately 7 feet [2.2 m] from the floor) plus the length of the bed. Use a fabric that looks good from both sides, either plain or a woven pattern, and is the same width or wider than the bed, so that it will not be necessary to join fabric widths.

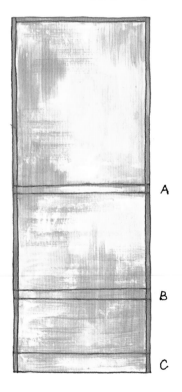

2 Cut the fabric to the width of the bed. Bind both long sides and the short side that goes down to the floor with bias binding (page 181).

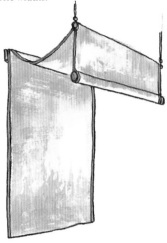

3 At point B make a casing in the fabric large enough to receive a ¾-inch- (2-cm-) diameter dowel. At point C (the unfinished end of the canopy), turn the hem up so that it is wide enough for another ¾-inch (2-cm) diameter dowel.

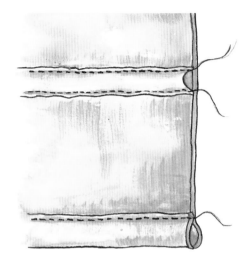

4 At point A sew the soft part of a strip of hook-and-loop tape, ½ inches (3.5 cm) in width, to the other side of the fabric across the width of the whole canopy. Screw a 1½ x ½ inch- (3.5 x 1 cm-) wooden batten to the wall at the correct height from which to hang the canopy. Staple the other part of the hook-and-loop tape to this wooden batten as shown below.

5 Feed the dowel through the casing at point B. It should protrude by 1 inch (2.5 cm) on either side of the canopy. Drill a small hole at each end of the dowel and attach two rings as shown. Thread the cords through the top rings. Attach the canopy to the wall with the hook-and-loop tape, and hold up the cords to calculate the exact position to screw two hooks into the ceiling to suspend the other end of the canopy. Feed the second dowel through the end casing in the hem. This should be cut to exactly the same width as the canopy.

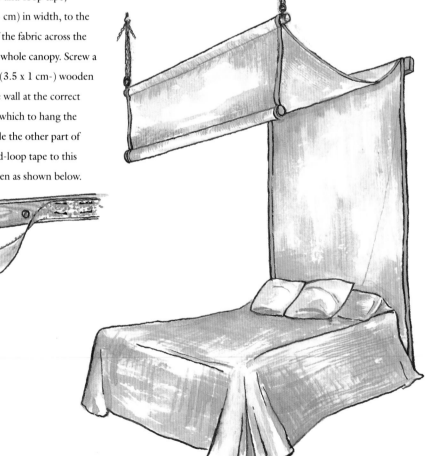

SEWING TECHNIQUES

The basic sewing methods shown here are not intended to be comprehensive, but they cover the most important techniques for making the curtains, draperies, and shades described in "Practicalities."

STITCHES

This range of stitches will enable you to achieve a professional finish when sewing any window treatment. Although much of the work is done by machine, there are places where hand stitching is essential. It allows for greater precision and hence better finished results. You can start and finish stitching with either a double backstitch or with a knot.

Running or Gathering Stitch

This hand-worked stitch is used mainly for gathering fabric or for basting. It is not a strong stitch, so it should not be used to sew seams. If a seam is too awkward to reach with a sewing machine, and you need to sew it by hand, you should use backstitches.

Secure the thread with a backstitch and sew small, regularly spaced stitches along the fabric. For basting, the stitches can be fairly large.

When using running stitches to gather a piece of fabric, such as for a gathered tieback, valance, or a simple decorative ruffle, sew two parallel lines of stitching approximately ¼ inch (5 mm) apart on either side of the seamline. Make sure that both threads are securely fastened at the starting point. Leave the finishing ends loose. Gather up the fabric as evenly as possible to the required length, sliding the fabric gently over the gathering threads. Secure the loose threads by twisting them in a figure eight around a pin and adjust the gathers if necessary.

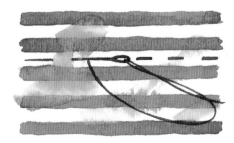

Backstitch

Working from right to left, insert the needle approximately ⅛ inch (3 mm) behind the spot where the thread came out. Bring the needle out again the same distance in front of this point. Continue by inserting the needle in the end of the last stitch.

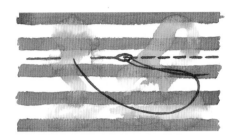

Catchstitch

This is a firm hemming stitch that is suitable for draperies and is used over any raw edge that will then be covered by another layer of fabric. Working from left to right of the material, secure the thread with a small stitch and bring the needle up through the fabric approximately ⅛ inch (3 mm) above the edge of the hem. Take the needle diagonally down to make a small backward stitch, from right to left, in the hem just below the edge. Bring the needle diagonally back to the fabric again and make another backward stitch in the fabric. Make sure that the thread is fairly loose while you work.

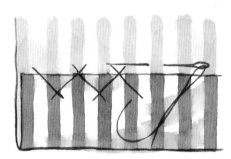

Lock Stitch

This is a particularly useful stitch, somewhat like catchstitch, although the thread is left very loose. It is used to hold linings and other fabric layers together where they must retain a degree of movement and flexibility.

1 After you have folded back and secured the lining or interlining to the main fabric with pins,
fold back the lining to the first row of pins. Secure the thread at the top and make a stitch through the folded lining and the main fabric, picking up only a few threads with each stitch.

2 Make the next stitch about 2 inches (5 cm) farther along and bring the needle out over the thread to produce a loop. Keeping the thread very loose, continue down the length of the row.

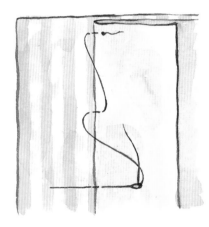

Slipstitch

This is often used to stitch the folded edge of a lining to the main fabric. Use a thread that matches the main fabric. Working from right to left, make a small stitch in the main fabric and insert the needle immediately into the fold as close as possible to the previous stitch. Pull the thread through. This should be done in one continuous movement.

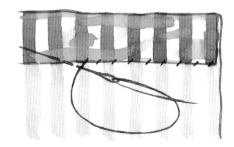

SEAMS

The look of your fabric furnishings will be marred by puckered or badly finished seams. Make sure that the raw edges are even before you start sewing, so that the seam allowances are the same.

Flat Seams

1 Pin, baste, and machine-stitch the right sides of the material together. Reverse the stitching at the ends of the seam to secure it. As a guide, you could insert horizontal pins ⅝–¾ inch (1.5–2 cm) from the raw edge and more pins at right angles, halfway between them. Machine-stitch, but remove the horizontal pins as the presser foot reaches them.

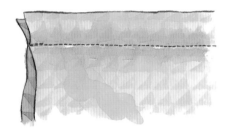

2 Remove all pins and basting, open out the seam, and then press open for a neat finish.

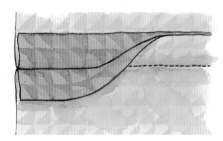

Curved Seams

Trimming curved seams serves to reduce bulk where the seams cannot be pressed open. Pin and stitch as usual but clip outward curves at intervals and cut V-shaped notches along an inward-curving seam. Press the seam open.

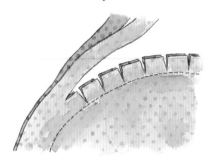

French Seams

This self-finishing seam encloses raw edges, but it can be bulky, so use it only on sheer or lightweight fabrics and only on straight edges.

1 With the wrong sides of the fabric together, sew a narrow seam. Trim off the seam allowance. Fold the fabric over the seam and press flat. Stitch again, about ½ inch (1 cm) from the first seam.

Lapped Seams

This seam is ideal if you wish to match the pattern on the right sides of two pieces of fabric.

1 Turn under one edge of the fabric by ½ inch (1 cm) and pin it in place over the other piece of fabric, matching the pattern where necessary.

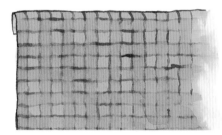

2 Pin and machine-stitch along the fold line on the right side of the fabric.

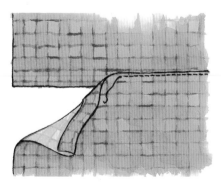

3 Sew another seam parallel to the first to catch down the raw edge underneath.

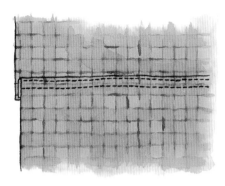

MITERING CORNERS

You will need to miter a corner when turning up a hem at a corner. In fact, mitering is the neatest way of working hem corners. This mitering method is also suitable for hems of unequal length, as is so often the case while making draperies where the bottom hem is deeper than the side hems. Borders and edgings also look much better when mitered.

1 Turn up the hems along the bottom and side edge of the fabric by the amount specified in the instructions. If you are basting the side hems first, do not pin and baste right up to the hem, so that you have enough fabric to fold over. Press and open out the folds. Fold in the corner diagonally so that the second fold lines match up. Press flat.

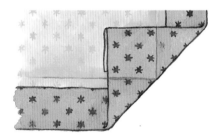

2 Trim down the corner between these matching points as shown below.

3 Fold the edges in place and slipstitch the seam, working inward toward each of the corners.

4 This method also works well for draperies that have side hems and a bottom hem of different depths. Simply slipstitch the corner hems where they do correspond.

BINDING

Binding is a simple yet effective method of finishing raw edges and also provides an attractive border for a drapery, shade, or other accessory. There are two types of binding: straight and bias. Both types are available ready-made, although in many cases you can achieve a more professional finish by making the binding yourself. On a curved or diagonal edge, bias binding must be used.

Applying Straight Binding

1 Fold and press the binding as shown and, with right sides together, place it against the raw edge of the main fabric. Machine-stitch the binding along the fold line nearer the edge.

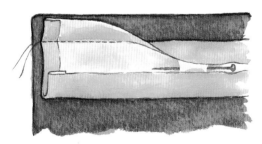

2 Fold the binding over the raw edge to the wrong side of the main fabric and slipstitch in place. Slipstitch the binding neatly at each end.

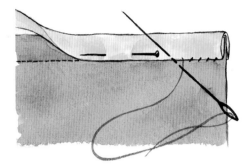

Bias Binding

1 Fold the piece of fabric so that the selvage is parallel to the weft, or cross grain. Press the fold and cut along it. Draw a series of lines parallel to the diagonal cut line, spacing them ½ inch (1 cm) wider than the finished binding. Cut along the lines.

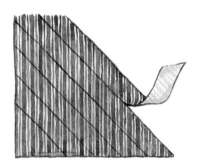

2 Place two strips at right angles and stitch together ¼ inch (5 mm) from the edge.

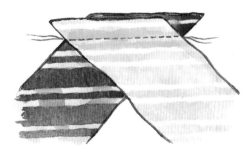

3 Press the seam open and trim away the points of fabric. Apply to the fabric as for straight binding.

Mitering Binding

1 Mitering binding enables you to apply it around a corner. Place binding against the edge of the fabric with right sides facing. Machine-stitch along one edge to the corner point of the seamline. At the corner, fold the binding back over the stitched length so that the fold is in line with the stitching. Stitch the binding along the second edge.

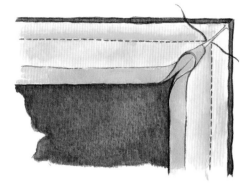

2 Continue to fold back the binding like this at each corner. Turn the binding over the raw edge of the fabric and hand-stitch the other side of the binding to the fabric. Press the corners into miters on both sides by tucking under the fabric.

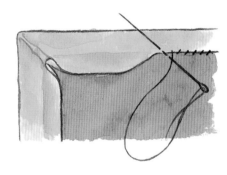

PIPING

Piping is made by inserting cord into binding strips. The width of the binding should equal the circumference of the cord plus 1¼ inches (3 cm) of seam allowance. Wrap the binding around the cord and pin it in place. Sew the fabric together close to the cord, using the zipper foot. Place the piping against the raw edge of the main fabric and stitch.

Glossary

Appliqué Applying a second layer of fabric onto a base cloth, usually with decorative stitching.

Architrave The molding around a window or doorway.

Backstitch A firm hand stitch that resembles machine stitching on the right side of the fabric and overlaps on the wrong side.

Balloon shade A shade consisting of vertical rows of horizontally gathered fabric that may be drawn up to form a series of ruches.

Basting Large straight stitches for temporarily fastening layers of fabric. The thread is usually made of cotton and worked in a loose stitch.

Bay window A window projecting from the wall to form an alcove.

Bias binding A strip of fabric cut obliquely from selvage to selvage for additional strength. Used to bind fabric edges and to enclose piping.

Bow window A bay window in the shape of a curve.

Bracket A decorative support, often made from metal or wood, that holds a curtain or drapery in place.

Braid A woven ribbon for trimming or edging draperies or accessories.

Brocade A woven fabric using silk, wool, cotton, or mixed fibers. Often washable.

Café curtain An informal curtain with a scalloped heading. Often hung halfway down the window.

Cascade The piece of fabric that falls from the end of a swag.

Catchstitch A hemming stitch that is used over any raw edge which is then covered by another fabric.

Chintz Glazed cotton in plain colors or prints. Ideal for curtains, draperies, valances, shades, and bed furnishings. Dry-clean only or the glaze will eventually wash out.

Cornice A horizontal molding at the top of a wall or a decorative board, often molded or painted, that is fixed to the top of the window.

Corona drape A drapery that hangs from a pole or a semicircular bracket (often known as a coronet) at the top of the bed.

Cotton A natural fiber made from the boll of the cotton plant to produce a strong durable yarn. There are a variety of cotton fabrics available, including Madras cotton, a fine striped Indian cotton, usually in bright colors, and cretonne, a heavy cotton cloth. Organdie is also made with cotton yarns.

Crewel Plain or woven cotton or linen with cream or multicolored embroidery that is usually in wool. Crewel is ideal for heavy curtains or draperies or for soft shades. It is often washable but you should check for color fastness first, particularly if the crewel-work is in wool.

Curtain An informal window covering, usually made with a casing, which slips over a rod. Curtains may also be hung from rings.

Damask A reversible figured woven fabric usually made from silk, satin, or linen. Dry-clean only.

Drapery Window covering with (usually) pleated headings which may be lined or unlined. They are usually hung from a traverse rod so that they can be drawn.

Facing A strip of fabric used to hide the raw edge of main fabric, especially on unlined curtains or draperies.

Figured material A fabric with a pattern formed by the structure of the weave.

Finial A decorative fixture attached to the end of a curtain or drapery rod or pole. Available in a range of styles.

Flat seam A simple seam for sewing two pieces of fabric together.

French seam A self-neatening seam to enclose raw edges. Use lightweight fabrics or if a seam will be visible.

Fringe A decorative edging with hanging threads or tassels.

Gathers Folds or puckers created by drawing on loosely stitched thread; hence, running stitch, which is used for gathering fabric or for basting.

Gimp A twist of fabric, sometimes stiffened with cord or wire.

Gingham A plain weave cotton cloth usually woven in stripes or checks. It is suitable for informal curtains.

Grain The pattern of lines on a fabric depending on the weave.

Heading The finish at the top of a curtain or drapery, ranging from simple gathers to pleats and swags. Although many heading styles can be achieved using pleater tapes, hand-sewn headings are more professional.

Hem The border or cut edge of cloth, usually turned under and sewn in place.

Holland linen A hard-wearing, fade-resistant fabric stiffened with oil or shellac. It is particularly useful for valances and shades. Holland can also be made from cotton.

Interfacing Special material for lining and stiffening. It is either sewn or ironed in place.

Interlining A soft but thick fabric in white or off-white that adds bulk to and improves the hang of draperies, valances, swags and cascades. Also acts as an extra layer of insulation. Often known as bump or domette. Dry-clean only.

Lambrequin An ornamental hanging that covers the upper part of a window or door.

Lapped seam A useful seam for matching the pattern on the right sides of two pieces of fabric.

Lawn A fine fabric made from linen or cotton.

Linen Fibers spun from flax to produce a strong but flexible fabric.

Lining Plain cotton with a slight satin weave originally only in white or off-white but now available in a range of colors. Clean as for main fabric but wash the lining with the fabric before making the curtains or draperies to prevent uneven shrinkage.

Lit à la polanaise Drapes that fall from a central point above a bed.

Lock stitch A loose stitch that allows for a degree of movement. Ideal for holding together fabrics, linings, and interlinings.

Miter The diagonal join of two pieces of fabric formed at a corner; hence mitered corners.

Muslin A sheer, strong but delicately woven fabric in white or off-white that can be dyed with pastel colors. Ideal for undercurtains and sheers. Most muslin can withstand a gentle wash but will sometimes shrink and need ironing in order to regain its shape.

Notch A small V-shaped cut in the edge of a fabric.

Passementerie A term to describe a range of decorative trimmings such as gimp, cord, beads, and braid.

Pleat A double fold or crease, pressed or stitched in place.

Pleat tape A tape that is purpose-made to create a particular heading styles.

Portière A curtain or drapery hung in a doorway.

Raw edge The cut edge of fabric, without selvage or hem.

Recess The area of wall around a window when it is set in from the main wall.

Rod casing A type of curtain heading in which a pocket of material is left open at both ends to receive a curtain rod or pole.

Roman shade A shade operated by vertical cords at the back. The fabric draws up into neat folds.

Ruffle A gathered strip of cloth used as a decorative trimming.

Satin A silk, cotton, or synthetic fabric with a smooth, glossy surface and a dull back. Suitable for curtains, valances, shades, and draperies. Wash or dry-clean.

Seam allowance The narrow strip of raw-edged fabric left when making a seam to allow for fraying.

Seamline The line formed when fabric pieces are stitched together.

Selvage The defined warp edge of the fabric, specially woven to prevent unraveling.

Silk A luxuriously strong fabric that is produced by silkworms. There are a variety of silks to choose from, including silk noil, a light- to medium-weight silk, which is ideal for interlining heavy draperies and for making lightweight curtains or draperies. Silk shantung, which has a rather dull appearance, is another light- to medium-weight silk suitable for curtains or draperies. Silks will also provide a further layer of insulation. Dry clean only.

Slipstitch Often used to stitch the folded edge of a lining to the main fabric. Use a color thread to match the main fabric.

Swag Fabric that hangs from two fixed points at the top of the window, and sweeps down in the center to create an elegant curve.

Taffeta A mixed-weave fabric, including silk and acetate, with a reflective sheen. Ideal for extravagant draperies. Dry-clean only.

Template A shape made of cardboard or paper and used to mark the specific outlines on a piece of fabric.

Tester A canopy over a four-poster bed; hence, a half-tester.

Tieback A band of fabric used to tie curtains or draperies to one side. Tiebacks may be as simple as a piece of ribbon or brocade or shaped in some way.

Toile A plain cloth or, when described as *toile de Jouy*, one that is embellished with pictorial scenes printed on cotton. Dry-clean only.

Traverse rod A rod with a cord at the side for drawing the curtain or drapery.

Undercurtain The curtain closest to the window in a treatment that includes at least two layers.

Valance A strip of fabric in a variety of styles. Run across the top of a window or along a bed, it is ideal for hiding any structural imperfections.

Velvet A rich fabric with a thick pile, usually made of cotton, silk, or nylon.

Voile A light, plain weave cotton or polyester fabric in a variety of single colors. Suitable for sheer curtains, valances, and bed drapes. Silk and wool voiles are ideal for fine draperies. Washable.

Weave The interlacing action that forms a piece of fabric.

Width The distance from selvage to selvage on any fabric.

Directory of Suppliers

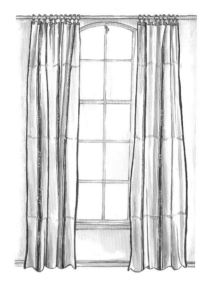

Items marked with an asterisk (*) are available only through architects and interior designers.

B & J Fabric
263 West 40th Street
New York, NY 10018
212-354-8150
*Natural fiber fabrics.
Call or write for samples.
Search and special-order
services.*

Boussac of France*
979 Third Avenue
New York, NY 10022
212-421-0534
*Cotton printed and woven
fabrics with coordinating
wallcoverings.*

Brunschwig & Fils*
979 Third Avenue
New York, NY 10022
*Wide range of printed and
woven fabrics in a variety of
natural fibers.*

Calico Corners
203 Gale Lane
Kennett Square, PA 19348
800-213-6366
*Over 100+ retail outlets that
discount fabrics. Custom work-
room services. Mail order. Catalog.*

Clarence House Fabrics, Ltd.*
211 East 58th Street
New York, NY 10022
212-752-2890
*Printed natural fiber fabrics based
on documents from the 15th-20th
centuries. Hand-woven textiles.*

Covington Fabrics*
15 East 26th Street
New York, NY 10010
212-689-2200
*Extensive range of classic and
fashion-forward fabrics.*

Cowtan & Tout, Inc*
979 Third Avenue
New York, NY 10022
212-753-488
*Traditional fabrics from silk
brocades to prints on linen.*

The Fabric Center
485 Electric Avenue
Fitchburg, MA 01420
508-343-4402
*A wide variety of decorator fabrics
at discounted prices.
Mail order. Catalog.*

Hinson & Co*
979 Third Avenue
New York, NY 10022
212-688-5538
*A variety of fabrics with an
emphasis on clean designs. There is
also a selection of coordinating
wall-coverings as well as a good
choice of decorative accessories
and trims.*

Keepsake Quilting
Route 25B
P.O. Box 1618
Center Harbor, NH 03226-1618
800-865-9458
*Good selection of lightweight
cottons. There is also a wide range
of threads as well as notions
available.
Mail order. Catalog.*

Oppenheim's
P.O. Box 29
120 East Main Street
North Manchester
IN 46962-0052
800-461-6728
*Country prints, mill remnants,
denim, chambray, flannels.
Swatches on request with stamped
self-addressed envelopes.
Mail order. Catalog.*

Pierre Deux
570 Madison Avenue
New York, NY 10021
212-570-9343
*French Provincial printed fabrics
from own workrooms and Les
Olivabes. Custom drapery service.
Unique trims.
Mail order. Catalog.*

F. Schumacher & Co.*
79 Madison Avenue
New York, NY 10016
800-552-9255
*Extensive selection of fabrics in
various fibers. There are also
coordinating trims available.*

Scalamandre Silk, Inc.*
950 Third Avenue
New York, NY 10022
718-361-8500
*Leading restorer of classic
document fabrics for historic
houses. There are also adaptations
available for home use. Trims,
wallpaper, custom carpets. Also
houses Museum of Textiles.*

Smith & Noble
P.O. Box 1387
Corona, CA 91718
800-248-8888
*Vertical and horizontal shades
and blinds in all materials,
Roman shades, cornice boxes.
Mail order. Catalog.*

Thai Silks!
252 State Street
Los Altos, CA 94022
800-722-7455
*Large selection of silk, velvet,
organza, jacquard, and taffeta.
There are also imported fabrics,
including batik.
Mail order. Catalog.*

Waverley Fabrics*
79 Madison Avenue
New York, NY 10016
212-213-7900
*Broad selection of printed and
woven fabrics in natural fibers.
There are also coordinating
accessories and wallpaper
borders.*

NOTIONS AND TRIMS

Clothilde, Inc.
2 Sew Smart Way
Stevens Point, WI 54481-8031
800-772-2891
*Discounted notions, trims,
threads, books, and videos for the
home sewer.
Mail order. Catalog.*

Conso Products
P.O. Box 326
Union, SC 29379
800-845-2431
*Enormous collection of decorative
trims, tassels, and fringes of all
types. Call for local distributor.*

Hollywood Trims
Prym-Dritz Corporation
P.O. Box 5028
Spartanburg, SC 29304
800-845-4948
*Rayon, cotton, and metallic trims,
cords, tassels, and thread.
Mail order. Catalog.*

Houlés, Inc.*
8584 Melrose Avenue
Los Angeles, CA 90069
310-652-6171
*Luxurious handmade imported
trimmings of all sorts. Hardware.*

Nancy's Notions
P.O. Box 683
Beaver Dam, WI 53916
800-833-0690
*Notions, trims, threads, books,
and videos for the home sewer.
Mail order. Catalog.*

C. M. Offray & Sons, Inc.
Route 24
P. O. Box 601
Chester, NJ 07930
908-879-4700
*Woven and wire-edge ribbons,
flowers, and bows. From fabric
and notion stores nationwide.*

Tinsel Trading Co.
47 West 38th Street
New York, NY 10018
212-730-1030
*Vintage to contemporary
trims, tassels, flowers, fringes,
buttons, cords, metallics, and
military trims.
Mail order. Catalog.*

CURTAIN HARDWARE

Country Curtains
The Red Lion Inn
Stockbridge, MA 01262
800-244-6020
*Extensive assortment of hardware.
There is a wide selection of fabric
and lace curtains on offer as well
as swags and other accessories.
Mail order. Catalog.*

Gige Interiors Ltd.
170 South Main Street
Yardley, PA 19067
215-493-8052
*Custom-made window treatments.
There is also a range of imported
and custom-embellished hardware
available.*

General Clutch Corp.
200 Harvard Avenue
Stamford, CT 06902
800-552-5100
*One-cord control system for blinds
and shades. The clutch allows the
cord to stop and hold the shade or
blind in place.
Mail order. Catalog.*

Kirsch
P.O. Box 0370
Sturgis, MI 49091
800-528-1407
*Enormous selection of curtain
and drapery hardware and rods.
Also fabric window coverings
and blinds.*

Rue de France
78 Thomas Street
Newport, RI 02840
800-777-0998
*All types of hardware available.
Specialities include Country
French lace. There is also a
selection of fabric curtains and
accessories available.
Mail order. Catalog.*

Springs Window Fashions
7549 Graber Road
Middleton, WI 53562
800-521-8071
*Vinyl, metal, and fabric vertical
and horizontal blinds and shades.
Fashion and pleated shades are
also available.
Mail order. Catalog.*

The Warm Company
954 East Union
Seattle, WA 98122
800-234-9276
*Insulated fabric for window shades.
Call for your nearest retail outlet.*

WINDOW HARDWARE

Blaine Window Hardware, Inc.
17319 Blaine Drive
Hagerstown, MD 21740
301-797-6500
*Over 40,000 replacement parts
for windows and patio doors.
Mail order. Catalog.*

Home Depot
*A wide selection of hardware
at discounted prices. Check local
telephone directory for the store
nearest you.*

Materials Unlimited
2 West Michigan Avenue
Ypsilanti, MI 48197
800-299-9462
*Antique and reproduction
window hardware. Antique
doorknobs to be used as tiebacks.
Mail order. Catalog.*

Renovator's Supply
P. O. Box 2515
Conway, NH 03818
800-659-0203
*Reproduction wooden architectural
details with a Country or
Victorian look.
Mail order. Catalog.*

Architects and Designers

The page numbers refer to
pictures of the main locations.

Andrew Arnott & Karin Shack
Art & Design
517 High Street
Prahran
Victoria 3181, Australia
Karin Shack and her husband,
Andrew Arnott, both have back-
grounds in design. Elegant simplicity,
the textural qualities of materials, and
an attention to detail characterize
their work. (page 49)

Ash Sakula Architects
38 Mount Pleasant
London WC1X OAN
A London-based firm of architects.
(page 130, left)

Charlotte Barnes Interiors
26 Stanhope Gardens
London SW7 5QX
An interior decorator, Charlotte
Barnes provides elegant, beautiful,
and practical solutions, tailored to
each client and property. (pages 29,
below; 36; 82, left; 100)

James Biber, AIA
Pentagram Architecture
204 Fifth Avenue
New York, New York 10010
An international design partnership,
specializing in architectural design
and interiors. (page 33)

Mary Bright
Since 1986, Mary Bright has focused
on designing draperies and other
related elements. She concentrates on
both the functional and aesthetic
attributes of a design. She has been
referred to as "the leading avant-
garde curtain designer in New York."
(pages 32-3; 34, above; 35)

Milly de Cabrol, Ltd.
150 East 72nd Street, Suite 2-C
New York, New York 10021
An Italian decorator now living in
New York, Milly de Cabrol has a wide
range of clients. She loves working
with color and mixing styles, such as
putting African, Moroccan, and
Indian objects and fabrics in a room
to add an exotic and unusual touch.
(page 29, above)

Carnachan Architects Limited
Architects, Interior Designers and
Landscape Architects
27 Bath Street
P.O. Box 37.717
Parnell
Auckland, New Zealand
This firm of architects is renowned
for its innovative, carefully designed,
and detailed work. (pages 113; 123,
right; 127, above)

Jacqueline Coumans
Le Décor Français
1006 Lexington Avenue
New York, New York 10021
In 1983, Jacqueline Coumans started
her own company importing fabric
from Europe and making items such
as draperies and pillows. (page 95)

Vincent Dané
Interior Design Antiques
50 Cranby Gardens
London SW7 3DE
Vincent Dané created a collection of
furnishing materials with Melissa
Wyndham. He now works as an
interior designer. (page 46, left)

Françoise Dorget
Caravane
6 rue Paveé
75004 Paris
Having developed a strong attraction
for unusual and exotic textiles,
Françoise Dorget developed a line of
printed and woven furnishing fabrics.
She established Caravane, which is a
gallery-boutique, to deal in antique
textiles and furniture. She has also
started a company called Etamine.
(pages 30-31; 60, left; 77, 129)

Timney Fowler Design Studio
29 Warple Way
London W3 ORF
This studio was founded in 1979 and
produces a collection of furnishings.
It has over two dozen collections of
fabrics and wallpapers. (page 50)

Pierre Frey (UK) Ltd.
251-253 Fulham Road
London SW3 6HY
Founded in 1935, the company is
now run by Patrick Frey. It specializes
in furnishing fabrics, both printed
and woven. (pages 23; 66; 139, right)

Christophe Gollut
Alistair Colvin Limited
116 Fulham Road
London SW3 6HU
Christope Gollut's trademark is rich, unusual rooms, with an undecorated look and a feeling of permanence. (pages 14-15; 44-45; 61; 99; 151)

Annie Har
Sunnit Architects
10 Attunga Lane
Mount Glorious
Queensland 4520, Australia
The location shown in the photograph is in Brisbane, and belongs to William Hayes and Annie Har. (page 116, below)

Kelly Hoppen Interiors
2 Alma Studios
32 Stratford Road
Kensington
London W8 6QF
Kelly Hoppen's style is uncluttered and effective, giving an impression of luxurious simplicity. She creates an impact by juxtaposing lavish fabrics with much humbler fabrics. (pages 10-11; 27; 37; 53; 69)

Stephanie Hoppen
17 Walton Street
London SW3 2HZ
An interior designer whose work reflects changing fashions. She regularly works in association with Doreen Scott, a curtain-designer. pages 10-13; 93, below; 153)

Interni Pty Ltd.
Interior Design Consultancy
15-19 Boundary Street
Rushcutter's Bay
Sydney 2011, Australia
Madeline Lester and Louise Bell are the directors of this company, which creates living areas, taking all aspects of the design process, including the architecture and window treatments, into account. (pages 55, below; 87, below left and above right)

IPL Interiors
Thames House
140 Battersea Park Road
London SW11 4NY
François Gilles and Dominique Lubar founded IPL Interiors in 1980. Their look is classic, but contemporary, with a continental touch and, often, an ethnic flavor. (pages 47, above; 52; 57, above; 80; 91; 110-11).

Jed Johnson & Associates
211 West 61st Street
New York, New York 10023
Jed Johnson began this interior design company in 1978. The firm specializes in residential commissions ranging from traditional design to a more modern vernacular under the design direction of Christine Cain and Arthur Dunnam. (pages 83; 134-5)

Larcombe & Solomon Architects
Level 3, 397 Riley Street
Surry Hills 2010
NSW, Australia
Caroline Larcombe and Nicholas Solomon both specialize in residential work. They are committed to making each project unique. (page 90, left and above right)

Khai Liew Design
166 Magill Road
Norwood
South Australia 5067, Australia
The photographs shown in the book are of Khai Liew's and Sue Kellet's house in Adelaide, Australia. (page 118-19)

Hilton McConnico
8 rue Antoine Panier
93170 Bagnolet, Paris
Currently a painter, stylist, decorator, photographer, and designer, Hilton McConnico lives in Paris. He has received numerous awards for his designs and his work has also been purchased by museums all over the world. (pages 2; 65; 70-71)

Frédéric Méchiche
4 rue de Thorigny
75003 Paris
With a passion for every historical period, from antiquity to the present day, Frédéric Méchiche is first and foremost an architect. His commissions have included castles and hotels in Britain as well as Greek villas and French houses. After several years designing for famous labels in Paris, he became the art director and costume designer for many well-known Truffaut films. He prefers to concentrate on the architecture, atmosphere, and objects of a design. (pages 16; 38-39; 105)

Andrew Parr
SJB Interior Design Pty Ltd.
Studio Southbank
5 Haig Street
South Melbourne 3205, Australia
Specializing in services in interior design, Andrew Parr, the managing director of SJB Interiors, works in association with Synman Justin Blalek Architects. The recipient of numerous design awards, he has also exhibited at Sotheby's Decorator Show House in 1996 and in the Royal Botanical Gardens in Melbourne, Australia. (page 86)

Campion A. Platt
641 Fifth Avenue
New York, New York 10022
Campion Platt runs an architecture and interior design practice, which specializes in designing, as well as furnishing, private residences. (pages 74-5)

Charles Rutherfoord
51 The Chase
London SW4 ONP
Trained in architecture and interiors, Charles Rutherfoord's work hinges on structural and sculptural concepts. He has a passion for unusual materials and color associations. (pages 76, above; 109, right)

John F. Saladino
305 East 63rd Street
New York, New York 10021
John Saladino's architectural and interior design practice started in 1972. With commissions throughout the United States, his work has won numerous awards for interior and furniture design. (pages 64; 120)

Henry Smith-Miller & Laurie Hawkinson, Architects
305 Canal Street
New York, New York 10013
A New York-based firm of architects, specializing in contemporary designs. (page 32, below)

Tony Suttle
Woods Baget Pty Ltd.
64 Marine Parade
Southport
Queensland 4000, Australia
Tony Suttle is an architect and interior designer. (page 48, left)

Emily Todhunter Interiors
The Studio House
31 Kenley Walk
Holland Park
London W11 4XG
Emily Todhunter has developed a range of styles to suit her clients' needs. (page 20, below)

Stephen Varady Architecture
Studio 5
102 Albion Street
Surry Hills
Sydney 2010, Australia
Stephen Varady is well-travelled, and this is reflected in his work, which explores form and new materials. (page 107, above left)

Vicente Wolf Associates, Inc.
333 West 39th Street
New York, New York 10018
This leading contemporary designer has designed interiors worldwide as well as home collections. (pages 4-5; 20-21; 63; 72; 122; 131)

Picture Credits

All photographs are by James Merrell unless specified.

ar = architect d = designer (s) a = above t = top
be = below b = bottom l = left r = right c = center

Endpapers James Merrell; **1** Charles Chauliaguet and
Françoise Dorget's apartment in Paris by Caravane; **2** Hilton
McConnico's house near Paris; **3** Sue and Andy A'Court's
apartment in Blackheath, London; **4-5** Shelly Washington's
apartment (*d.* by Vicente Wolfe); **6 a. curtain d.** Mary Bright;
6 be. d. Vincent Dané; **7 a. d.** Françoise Dorget, Caravane;
7 be. curtain d. Mary Bright; **9** Elizabeth Whiting &
Associates/Jean-Paul Bonhommet; **10-13** an apartment in
London (designed by Stephanie Hoppen and executed by
Doreen Scott); **14-15** an apartment in London
(*d.* Christophe Gollut); **16** Frédéric Méchiche's house near
Toulon; **17** Arcaid/ Richard Bryant/Goethe's Garden
house, Weimar, Germany; **18-19** Sue and Andy A'Court's
apartment in Blackheath, London; **20 a. ar.** Campion A.
Platt; **20 be.** an apartment in London (*d.* Emily Todhunter);
20-21 Amy & Richard Sachs' apartment in New York (*d.*
Vicente Wolfe); **22 a.** Milly de Cabrol's apartment in New
York; **22 be.** Mr. & Mrs. Patrick Frey's house in Paris; **23**
Mr. & Mrs. Patrick Frey's house in Paris; **24 l. & a.c.**
Vincent Dané's house near Biarritz; **24 b.c. & r.** an
apartment in New York (*d.* Jacqueline Coumans, Le Décor
Français with the help of Olivier Gelbsmann); **25 a.l.**
François Gilles & Dominique Lubar, IPL Interiors; **25 b.l.**
Hilton McConnico's house near Paris; **25 r.** Mr. & Mrs.
Patrick Frey's house in Paris; **27** Kelly Hoppen's apartment
in London; **28** Dominique Vorillon/Chris Coleman Design;
29 a. Milly Cabrol's apartment in New York; **29 b. d.**

Charlotte Barnes; **30-31** Charles Chauliaguet and Françoise
Dorget's apartment in Paris by Caravane; **32 curtain
d.** Mary Bright; **32 b. ar.** Henry Smith-Miller & Laurie
Hawkinson, **curtain d.** Mary Bright; **33** an apartment in
New York (*d.* James Biber of Pentagram with curtain design
by Mary Bright); **34 a. curtain d.** Mary Bright; **34 b.**
Charles Chauliaguet and Françoise Dorget's apartment in
Paris by Caravane; **35 ar.** Ogawa Depardon (**curtain d.**
Mary Bright); **36 d.** Charlotte Barnes; **37** Kelly Hoppen's
apartment in London; **38-39** Frédéric Méchiche's house
near Toulon; **40** Paul Ryan/ International Interiors (*d.* Sasha
Waddell); **41 l.** a room in Stephanie Hoppen's London
apartment (designed by Kelly Hoppen and Doreen Scott);
41 a.c. a house in London (*d.* Charles Rutherfoord); **41 b.c.
& r.** Sue and Andy A'Court's apartment in Blackheath,
London; **42 a.** Robert Harding Picture Library/Homes &
Gardens ©IPC Magazines/ Jeremy Young; **42 b. d.** Roger
Banks-Pye; **42-43** Vincent Dané's house near Biarritz; **43**
Kelly Hoppen's apartment in London; **44-45** Christophe
Gollut's apartment in London; **46 l.** Vincent Dané's house
near Biarritz; **46 r.** Khai & Sue Kellet; **47 a. & be.r** François
Gilles & Dominique Lubar, IPL Interiors; **47 b.l.** Mr. &
Mrs. Patrick Frey's house in Paris; **48 l. & a.r.** Tony Suttle's
house in Brisbane; **48 be.r.** Andrew Arnott and Karin
Schack's house in Melbourne; **49** Andrew Arnott and Karin
Schack's house in Melbourne; **50** Sue Timney's house in
London (*d.* Timney-Fowler Ltd.); **50-51** Sue Timney's
house in London, (*d.* Timney Fowler Ltd); **51** an apartment
in London (*d.* Nigel Greenwood); **52** an apartment in Lon-
don (*d.* François Gilles & Dominique Lubar, IPL Interiors);
53 Kelly Hoppen's apartment in London **54 l. & a.r.** Kelly
Hoppen's apartment in London; **54 be.r.** Christian

Sarramon; **55 a.** Christian Sarramon; **55 be.** Interni Interior
Design Consultancy; **56 a.l.** Deidi von Schaewen (*d.*
Christian Astuguevielle); **56 a.r.** Dominique Vorillon/
Holden/Dupuy Design; **56 be.** David George; **57 a.** a house
in London (*d.* François Gilles & Dominique Lubar, IPL
Interiors); **57 be.** Agence Top/Pascal Chevlier (*d.* Lilian
Williams); **58** Tim Street-Porter (*d.* Kathryn Ireland); **59 a.l.**
Paul Ryan/International Interiors; **59 a.c.** Vincent Dané's
house near Biarritz; **59 a.r.** Marie Claire Maison/ Christophe
Dugied/Josée Postic; **59 b.l.** Christophe Dugied (E. van der
Straten); **60 l.** Charles Chauliaguet and Françoise Dorget's
apartment in Paris by Caravane; **60 r.** a house in London (*d.*
Christophe Gollut); **61** a house in London (*d.* Christophe
Gollut); **62 a.l.** Sue Timney's house in London (*d.* Timney-
Fowler Ltd.); **62 a.r.** The Interior Archive/James Mortimer;
62 b.l. an apartment in London (*d.* Charles Rutherfoord);
62 b.r. Arcaid/ Jeremy Cockayne (**ar.** Yann Weymouth); **63**
Shelly Washington's apartment in New York (*d.* Vicente
Wolfe); **64** John F. Saladino's apartment in New York; **65**
Hilton McConnico's house near Paris; **66-67** Mr. & Mrs.
Patrick Frey's house in Paris; **67** Dennis Krukowski; **68 a.**
Charles Rutherfoord's house in London; **68 b.l.** Mr. & Mrs.
Patrick Frey's house in Paris; **68 b.r.** Linda Trahair's house in
Bath; **69** Kelly Hoppen's apartment in London; **70-71**
Hilton McConnico's house near Paris; **72** Shelly Washing-
ton's apartment in New York (*d.* Vicente Wolfe); **73 l.** Amy
and Richard Sachs' apartment in New York (*d.* Vicente
Wolfe); **73 c.** Jean-Pierre Godeaut; **73 r. ar.** Campion A.
Platt; **74-75** an apartment in New York (**ar.** Campion A.
Platt); **76 a.** an apartment in London (*d.* Charles
Rutherfoord); **76 be.** Charles Chauliaguet and Françoise
Dorget's apartment in Paris by Caravane; **77** Charles

Chauliaguet and Françoise Dorget's apartment in Paris by *Caravane*; **78 l. & be.r.** Nigel Greenwood's apartment in London; **78 a.r.** Elizabeth Whiting & Associates/ Tim Street-Porter (*d.* Annie Kelly); **79** Nigel Greenwood's apartment in London; **80** a house in London (*d.* François Gilles & Dominique Lubar, IPL Interiors); **81 a & c.l.** Amy & Richard Sachs' apartment in New York (*d.* Vicente Wolfe); **81 be.l.** *d.* François Gilles & Dominique Lubar, IPL Interiors; **81 r.** Undine Prohl/Jim Jennings; **82 l.** *d.* Charlotte Barnes; **82 a.c.** an apartment in London (designed by Stephanie Hoppen and executed by Doreen Scott); **82 a.r.** an apartment in New York (*d.* Christine Cain of Jed Johnson & Associates and Sally McSween Ward); **82 be.r.** Dominique Vorillon (*d.* Denise Domergne); **83** an apartment in New York (*d.* Christine Cain of Jed Johnson & Associates and Sally McSween Ward); **84 a. & be.l.** Dominique Vorillon/ Goodman/Charlton Design; **84 be.r.** Tomasz Starzewski's apartment in London; **85** Tomasz Starzewski's apartment in London; **86** Andrew Parr's house in Melbourne; **87 a.l. & be.r.** Diane Atkinson and Patrick Hughes' flat in London (*d.* Michael Green of Green Homan, curtains by Timney-Fowler Ltd.); **87 be.l. & a.r.** Interni Interior Design Consultancy; **88 a.** an apartment in New York (*ar.* Campion A. Platt); **88 be.** Sarah Elson's house in London; **88-89** Paul Ryan/International Interiors (*d.* Bernardo Urquita); **89 a.** David Phelps/ courtesy *First for Women* Magazine; **89 be.l.** Interni Interior Design Consultancy; **89 be.r.** Amy & Richard Sachs' apartment in New York (*d.* Vicente Wolfe) **90 l. & a.r.** Larcombe and Solomon; **90 c. & be.r.** a house in London (*d.* François Gilles & Dominique Lubar, IPL Interiors); **91** a house in London (*d.* François Gilles & Dominique Lubar, IPL Interiors); **92** an apartment in London (*d.* Charles Rutherfoord); **93 a.l.** Vincent Dané's house near Biarritz; **93 a.r. & be.** an apartment in London (designed by Stephanie Hoppen and executed by Doreen Scott); **94 a.l. & r.** an apartment in London (designed by Stephanie Hoppen and executed by Doreen Scott); **94 be.l.** an apartment in New York (*d.* Milly de Cabrol); **95** an apartment in New York (*d.* Jacqueline Coumans, *Le Décor Français* with the help of Olivier Gelbsmann); **96** Sue Timney's house in London (*d.* Timney-Fowler Ltd.); **96-97** an apartment in London (*d.* François Gilles & Dominique Lubar, IPL Interiors); **97 a.l.** Mr. & Mrs. Patrick Frey's house in Paris; **97 a.r.** an apartment in London (*d.* François Gilles & Dominique Lubar, IPL Interiors); **98 a.l. & be.** Sue & Andy A'Court's apartment in Blackheath, London; **98 a.r.** Christophe Gollut's apartment in London; **99** Christophe Gollut's apartment in London; **100** *d.* Charlotte Barnes; **101 a.l. & r.** Tomasz Starzewski's apartment in London; **101 be.l.** David Phelps (*d.* Pat Guthman, Southport Conneticut); **102 a.** Dominique Vorillon (*d.* Madeline Stuart) **102 be.** Tim Street-Porter (*d.* Brian Murphy); **102-103** Frédéric Méchiche's house near Toulon; **103 a.** Ivan Terestchenko (*d.* Agnes Comar); **103 be.** Solvi Dos Santos; **104 a.l.** The Interior Archive/Tim Clinch; **104 be.l.** Paul Ryan/ International Interiors (*d.* Michael Trapp); **104 r.** David Phelps; **105** Frédéric Méchiche's house near Toulon;

106 l. Shelly Washington's apartment in New York (*d.* Vicente Wolfe); **106 r.** a house, London (*d.* François Gilles & Dominique Lubar, IPL Interiors); **107 a.l.** Amanda and Andrew Manning's apartment in Sydney (*d.* Stephen Varady); **107 be.l. d.** Interni Interior Design Consultancy; **107 r.** Roger & Fay Oates' House in Hereford- shire; **108 l. d.** Cath Kidston; **108 a.r.** Arcaid/Richard Bryant (*ar.* TSAO McKown); **108 c. & be.r.** Kelly Hoppen's apartment in London; **109 l.** Sarah Elson's house in London; **109 r.** an apartment in London (*d.* Charles Rutherfoord); **110 a.** Elizabeth Whiting & Associates/ Jean-Paul Bonhommet; **110 be.** Amy & Richard Sachs' apartment in New York (*d.* Vicente Wolfe); **110-1 111** a house in London (*d.* François Gilles & Dominique Lubar, IPL Interiors); **112 a.** Paul Ryan/International Interiors (*d.* Ken Foreman); **112 c.** Interni Interior Design Consultancy; **112 be.** Elizabeth Whiting & Associates/ Brian Harrison (*d.* Katie Large); **113** Robyn & Simon Carnachan's house in Auckland; **114** Andrew Parr's house in Melbourne; **115 l.** Interni Interior Design Consultancy; **115 r.** Paul Ryan/ International Interiors (*d.* John F. Saladino); **116 a.l.** a house, London (*d.* François Gilles & Dominique Lubar, IPL Interiors); **116 a.r. & be.** William Hayes & Annie Har's house near Brisbane; **117** a house, London (*d.* François Gilles & Dominique Lubar, IPL Interiors); **118-119** Khai Liew and Sue Kellet's house in Adelaide; **120** John F. Saladino's apartment, New York; **121** above left John F. Saladino's apartment, New York; **121** below Amy & Richard Sachs' apartment, New York (*d.* Vicente Wolfe); **122** Vicente Wolfe's apartment, New York; **123 a.l.** Amy & Richard Sachs' apartment, New York (*d.* Vicente Wolfe); **123 be.l.** Elizabeth Whiting & Associates/Jean-Paul Bonhommet; **123 r.** Robyn & Simon Carnachan's house in Auckland; **124** an apartment in New York (*d.* Jacqueline Coumans, Le Décor Français with the help of Olivier Gelbsmann); **124-125** Mr. & Mrs. Patrick Frey's house in Paris; **125 l.** Interni Interior Design Consultancy; **125 r.** an apartment in London (*d.* François Gilles & Dominique Lubar, IPL Interiors); **126 l.** Robyn & Simon Carnachon's house in Auckland; **126 a.r.** Jolie and Petrea Grant's house in Brisbane; **126 be.r.** Christian Sarramon/Alan Franchet; **127 a.l. & r.** Robyn & Simon Carnachon's house in Auckland; **127 c.l. & be.** an apartment, London (*d.* François Gilles & Dominique Lubar, IPL Interiors); **128 a.l.** John Raab's apartment in London; **128 a.r. & be.** Sue Timney's house in London (*d.* Timney-Fowler Ltd.); **129** Charles Chauliaguet and Françoise Dorget's apartment in Paris by *Caravane*; **130 l. & be.r.** an apartment in London (*d.* Ash Sakula Architects); **130 a.r. d.** Interni Interior Design Consultancy; **131** Vicente Wolfe's apartment in New York; **132 a.** an apartment in London (*d.* François Gilles & Dominique Lubar, IPL Interiors); **132 be.l.** Elizabeth Whiting & Associates/Spike Powell (*theatre d.* James Merifield); **132 be.r.** Bellevue Homestead, Coominya, a NT of Queensland Property; **132-133** an apartment in London (*d.* François Gilles & Dominique Lubar, IPL Interiors); **133** an apartment, in London (designed by Stephanie Hoppen and executed by Doreen Scott); **134 a.** Sue and Andy

A'Court; **134 be. d.** Kelly Hoppen; **134-135** an apartment, New York (*d.* Christine Cain of Jed Johnson & Associates and Sally McSween Ward); **136 a. d.** Kelly Hoppen; **136 c.** David Phelps (*d.* Max King); **136 be.** a room in Stephanie Hoppen's London apartment (designed by Kelly Hoppen and Doreen Scott); **137** Charles Chauliaguet and Françoise Dorget's apartment in Paris by *Caravane*; **138 t. & be.r. curtain d.** Mary Bright; **138 a.l.** Abode/Ian Parry; **138 c.l. d.** Vicente Wolfe; **138 a.r.** designed by Stephanie Hoppen and executed by Doreen Scott; **138-139 d.** François Gilles & Dominique Lubar, IPL Interiors; **139 c.l. & r.** Mr. & Mrs. Patrick Frey's house in Paris; **139 be.l. d.** John F. Saladino; **140 l.** Christian Sarramon; **140 r. d.** Vicente Dané; **141 a.l. d.** Vincent Dané; **141 a.r. d.** Vicente Wolfe; **141 c.l. d.** Hilton McConnico; **141 b.r.** The Interior Archive/ Simon Brown; **142 a.l.** Michael Garland (*d.* Fabbyo); **142 a.r. d.** Cath Kidston; **142 be.l.** Paul Ryan/International Interiors/Frances Halliday; **142 be.r.** designed by Stephanie Hoppen and executed by Doreen Scott; **143 a.l.** Sarah Elson; **143 a.r.** Sue and Andy A'Court; **143 c.l.** Yves Duronsoy; **143 be.l.** Marie Claire Maison/Nicolas Tosni/ Julie Borgeaud; **143 b.r.** designer Jacqueline Coumans, *Le Décor Français*, **144** a house in Toulon (*d.* Frédéric Méchiche); **145 a.l. & be.l. d.** Katrin Cargill; **145 r.** Arcaid/Richard Bryant (*interior d.* David Richmond Byers III); **147** Kelly Hoppen's apartment in London; **148** Sue Timney's house in London (*d.* Timney-Fowler Ltd.); **149 l. & a.r.** a house in London (*d.* François Gilles & Dominique Lubar, IPL Interiors); **149 be.r.** Sue Timney's house, London (*d.* Timney-Fowler Ltd.); **150 a.** a house in London (*d.* Christophe Gollut); **150 be.** Tomasz Starzewski's apartment in London; **150-151** Christophe Gollut's apartment in London; **152 a.l.** The Interior Archive/Tim Clinch; **152 a.r. d.** Charlotte Barnes; **152 be.l.** Christian Sarramon; **152 be.r. d.** Charles Rutherfoord; **153** designed by Stephanie Hoppen and executed by Doreen Scott; **154 l.** Guy Bouchet; **154 a.r.** Sue and Andy A'Court; **154-155** The Interior Archive/James Mortimer; **155 a. & be. d.** Kelly Hoppen; **155 c** Elizabeth Whiting & Associates/Jean-Paul Bonhommet; **156 l.** Sue and Andy A'Court's home in Blackheath, London; **156 a.r.** Jerome Darblay; **156 be.r. d.** Milly de Cabrol; **157 l. d.** Jacqueline Coumans, *Le Décor Français*, **157 r.** Alan & Hepzibah's house in Sussex, England; **158 a.l.** Dennis Krukowski (*d.* Irvine & Fleming); **158 a.c. d.** Charlotte Barnes; **158 c.l. d.** Tomasz Starzewski; **158 r.a. & c.** Christophe Gollut; **158 be.** Bellevue Homestead, Coominya, a NT of Queensland Property; **159 a.l. d.** Timney-Fowler Ltd.; **159 a.r. d.** François Gilles and Dominique Lubar, IPL Interiors; **159 c. d.** Katrin Cargill; **159 c.r. d.** Christophe Gollut; **159 be.l. & be.c. d.** François Gilles & Dominique Lubar, IPL Interiors; **159 be.r.** designed by Stephanie Hoppen and executed by Doreen Scott; **160 a.l.** Milly de Cabrol; **160 a.r.** John F. Saladino; **160 be.l.** Hilton McConnico; **160 be.r. d.** Campion A. Platt; **161 a.l.** Sarah Elson; **161 a.r. d.** Vicente Wolf; **161 be.l.** designed by Stephanie Hoppen and executed by Doreen Scott; **161 be.r.** Françoise Dorget's apartment; **162** Milly de Cabrol's apartment in NY.

Index

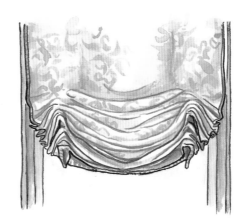

Acknowledgments

Author's acknowledgments: Writing a book on such a vast subject is a daunting task. However, the writing of *Curtains: A Design Source Book* was made much easier by all the help that I was given by those who know much more than I do. I would like to thank Corleen Rathbone, in particular, who is an exceptional curtain-maker and was more than generous with her time and knowledge. I would also like to thank everyone at Ryland, Peters & Small, especially Caroline Davison, Ingunn Jensen, and Nadine Bazar who all seemed to go out of their way to make the process as painless as possible.

Publisher's acknowledgments: The publishers would also like to thank those architects, designers, and owners who gave permission for photography of their work and homes for this book.